CW01647934

# ENGLISH FOR BUSINESS

Barbara Campbell

THOMSON™

**English for Business**
*Barbara Campbell*

Published by arrangement with Chambers Harrap Publishers Ltd.



**Publisher/Global ELT:** *Christopher Wenger*
**Executive Marketing Manager, Global ELT/ESL:** *Amy Mabley*

Printed in Croatia by Zrinski d.d
1 2 3 4 5 6 7 8 9 10 06 05 04 03 02 01



For more information contact Heinle, 25 Thomson Place, Boston, MA 02210 USA, or you can visit our Internet site at http://www.heinle.com



A CIP catalogue record for this book is available from the British Library.



**13 digit ISBN: 978 1 84480 528 0**
**10 digit ISBN: 1 84480 528 X**

Typeset by Chambers Harrap Publishers Ltd

# Contents

# Introduction

*English for Business* aims to help learners of English to operate with more confidence in the world of business. It is suitable for those studying in business-related courses, as well as for those who are already established in their careers.

The book covers a wide range of topics, both functional and factual. On the functional side, subjects such as 'essential language of negotiations' and 'language for business correspondence' are treated. On the factual side, users can expand their vocabulary by exploring such areas as employment, marketing, and computers and the Internet.

Language points and vocabulary are presented as follows:

- Key-word boxes highlight the vocabulary to be treated in the following section, enabling users to quickly identify the words they need to learn.
- 'Word-partnership' boxes show collocations, helping learners to expand their knowledge of how words work together.
- Information boxes give useful tips on important language points and common errors.
- 'Essential language' lists give hundreds of useful phrases for use in a wide variety of situations.
- Dialogues show language in context.
- Sample letters, faxes, memos, reports and e-mails give users models for a wide range of written material that they may need to produce.

We hope that people from all kinds of business-related backgrounds will enjoy using this book, and that it will help them to develop further in their particular areas of interest, from telephoning and writing e-mails, to negotiating and writing financial reports.

# 1

# Organizations

## What do we mean by 'organization'?

A business organization can be defined as a firm, a company, a business or a corporation that makes, buys or sells goods, or provides services, to make a profit. The words **firm**, **company**, **business** and **corporation** are often used interchangeably. The word **enterprise** is also sometimes used in the same way.

*I am happy to say the **firm** has made excellent progress this year.*
*She works for a biotechnology **company**.*
*The factory has been bought by a local packaging **business**.*
*A large American **corporation** has invested heavily in the project.*
*Starting up an **enterprise** of that type requires huge investment in plant and machinery.*

## The life of a business

The phrases below are frequently used to talk about the life of a company:

| | |
|---|---|
| set up in business | run a business |
| set up a business | do business |
| establish a business | go out of business |
| be in business | close down a business |

There are various expressions which are used to talk about starting a business, for example **set up in business**, **set up a business**, and **establish a business**. Once a business has been established it is usual to talk about **being in business** or **running a business**, ie. organizing, or being in charge of, a company.

To **do business** means to trade or deal with someone, for example a company or country.

When a company is not successful, it may be forced **go out of business**. If the decision is made, for whatever reason, to stop trading, the business may **close down**.

*Before **setting up in business** they carried out thorough market research.*
*The company **was set up** in 1972.*
*Her grandfather **established a small business** at the end of the war.*
*They've **been in business** together since 1994.*
*The same family has **run** this successful **whisky distillery** for most of this century.*
*If you are interested in **doing business** with Chinese companies, contact the Department of Trade for information.*
*Many small shops have **gone out of business** since the arrival of the large supermarket chains.*
*The factory was **closed down** due to increased production costs.*

## Expansion and change

The economic climate, as well as decisions taken by the owners of a company, affect how it grows and changes. The words below describe some of the changes that may take place.

| | |
|---|---|
| expand | branch out (into a particular area) |
| specialize (in something) | privatize (a company) |
| diversify | nationalize (a company) |

### expand
to grow and develop in a particular area: *Texaco expanded into oil production in the early part of this century.*

### specialize (in something)
to focus on, or to give more attention or resources to, something: *The firm specializes in youth travel and adventure holidays.*

### diversify
to begin to produce a wider range of goods or services: *The company diversified in the 1960s, and started producing food products as well as tobacco.*

**branch out (into a particular area)**
to expand into a new area of business: *We all agree on the need to branch out into sportswear and equipment.*

**privatize (a company)**
to sell a state-owned company into private ownership: *British European Airways was privatized in 1987.*

**nationalize (a company)**
to sell a privately-owned company into state ownership: *In 1938 the British Government nationalized two airlines to form BOAC.*

## Word partnerships: business

These words often occur after the word business:

| | |
|---|---|
| business... | community<br>school<br>studies<br>administration<br>partners<br>plan<br>trip<br>card |

The term **business community** refers to the organizations and people involved in business.

A **business school** is a college or part of a university where courses on business subjects are taught. **Business studies** is the name given to a course which teaches business-related subjects.

The process of running a company is called **business administration**; the people who own a business together are **business partners**. They may put together a document showing details of how they aim to run the company, expand, introduce new product lines, and so on. This document is known as a **business plan**.

You may have to make a **business trip** (a visit to clients, suppliers or other business contacts which takes you away from home). Most people working in business carry a supply of **business cards**. These are small cards showing a person's name, position and company name.

*Members of the **business community** are unhappy about government proposals to increase corporation tax.*

*MBA courses are now being offered in most **business schools.***

*With a degree in* ***business studies****, she hopes to find work in an overseas corporation.*
*If you study for a Masters in* ***Business Administration*** *(MBA), you will learn how to run a company.*
*Due to expansion, we are looking for new* ***business partners*** *to join our company.*
*I have an appointment with the bank manager to discuss our start-up* ***business plan****.*
*The job will require frequent* ***business trips*** *to the Far East.*
*Give me a call if you need anything; here's my* ***business card****.*

## Word partnerships: corporate

**Corporate** means 'related to a corporation or corporations'. The following words often occur after the word **corporate**:

| | |
|---|---|
| corporate ... | finance<br>restructuring<br>image<br>culture<br>responsibility<br>planning<br>strategy |

**Corporate finance** refers to the management activity and skills required to raise money and use that money in a company. **Corporate restructuring** takes place when major changes are made to the structure of a company or group of companies.

The way a company is seen by the public is its **corporate image**, while its **corporate culture** refers to its values and ways of doing things, unique to each company or group of companies. A company's role in relation to the effects of its activities on the community and the environment is known as its **corporate responsibility**.

**Corporate planning** is a broad term referring to decisions about the goals and future activities of the company, while **corporate strategy** refers to decisions about how to achieve the aims and targets put forward in plans.

*His experience in* ***corporate finance****, risk management in particular, makes him very suitable for this position.*
*Two subsidiary companies will be sold off as part of the* ***corporate restructuring*** *plan.*

*In an effort to improve its* ***corporate image****, the company launched a new public relations campaign.*
*Their* ***corporate culture*** *emphasizes the need for continuous improvement in customer service.*
*The idea of* ***corporate responsibility*** *is now taken seriously by an increasing number of companies and governments.*
*The next* ***corporate planning*** *meeting will be held on July 12 at Head Office. We will discuss our long-term objectives.*
*The board will be finalizing its* ***corporate strategy*** *next week.*

## The business organization and the economy

Different types of business fall into specific areas of activity. For example, a business may make things, such as furniture or cars, or it may sell items that have been produced by someone else. In addition, a company may be owned by the state, or by private individuals. The basic terms below will help you talk about how a company fits into the economy.

| | |
|---|---|
| sector | public sector |
| industry | service sector |
| private sector | manufacturing sector |

### sector
a part of the economy (usually occurs after 'private' or 'public', but is sometimes used in the same way as 'industry'): *French hypermarket companies have stepped up their operations in the Spanish retail sector.*

### industry
organized activity producing goods or services, for example food, banking, construction, steel, tobacco, biotechnology: *The organic food industry has seen rapid growth in the past five years.*

### private sector
privately-owned and -run companies: *Businesses in the private sector have been hit with job losses.*

### public sector
state-owned and -run organizations, eg. government departments, and nationalized industries, such as the postal service: *Public sector pay is expected to rise by only 3 per cent over*

*the next year.* ❑ *Thousands of job losses are expected in the public sector.*

### service sector
all the companies which provide services in areas such as tourism, banking and finance, communications, wholesale and retail trade: *Analysts predict continued growth in the service sector, particularly in tourism and car-hire.*

### manufacturing sector
all the companies which assemble components into finished products, or which make goods from raw materials: *In Europe, the manufacturing sector has been shrinking steadily, while the number of service sector jobs has increased.*

> ⓘ **Industry** and **sector** are sometimes used with the same meaning, eg. *the retail sector, the retail industry.*

## Ownership

A private business is a company which is owned by individuals or another company. In **unlimited liability companies** the owners are personally and entirely liable for the debts of the company. This means they may lose their personal assets (for example, their house or their car) if the company is in financial difficulties. In a **limited liability company** the owners are liable only for the amount of money they have invested in the business.

Different countries have different types of business organization. Here we look at the main UK and US types.

### *Unlimited liability companies*

| | |
|---|---|
| **sole trader**<br>**sole proprietorship** | **partnership**<br>**general partnership** |

### sole trader (*BrE*)
### sole proprietorship (*AmE*)
a type of business organization owned and run by one person: *As a sole trader, she works long hours in her hairdressing business. Being the owner of a sole proprietorship leaves you with little free time.*

**partnership (*BrE*)**
**general partnership (*AmE*)**
a firm run by two or more partners; typical examples are estate agents, accountants, architects, management consultants: *The partnership collapsed as a result of the criminal activities of one of the partners.*

## *Limited liability companies*

| | |
|---|---|
| private limited company | public limited company |
| limited liability company | listed company |

**private limited company (*BrE*)**
**limited liability company (*AmE*)**
a company which has shareholders (people who own the wealth of a company) but which cannot offer its shares to the public. UK companies of this type have 'Ltd.' in the name: *The bank was originally set up as a private limited company over a hundred years ago, but is now a public limited company.*

**public limited company (*BrE*)**
**listed company (*AmE*)**
a company whose shares (any of the equal parts into which the capital of a company is divided) can be bought and sold on the stock exchange: *She works as an Executive Director of one of the biggest listed companies in the US.* ❑ *Shareholders in a public limited company (plc) are invited to the company's annual general meeting.*

ⓘ A public limited company is privately owned. It is not run by the state.

- Do not use the word **society** to talk about companies in general.
- Note that a **building society** is a type of lending institution in the UK.

## Other forms of organization

You may come across other forms of organization. The following three are among the most common:

| franchise | co-operative | non-profit organization |
|---|---|---|

**franchise**
a business arrangement in which one party (the franchisee) pays for the right to use the name, and sell the products of, another company (the franchiser): *Many of the shops in the main street are run as franchises.*

**co-operative**
an association formed for a particular purpose, eg. to give better service to its members, and in which each member has an equal vote: *The largest co-operative in the country was set up in 1989 to enable its members to buy paper in large quantities at low prices.*

**non-profit organization**
an organization, usually a charity, that raises funds and offers products and services, but does not have to make a profit to stay in business: *Oxfam is a non-profit organization which operates to help the world's poor.*

## Relationships

As businesses expand they may buy shares (see chapter 11) in other companies, or join with other companies for a particular purpose. The words below describe the relationships these companies can have with one another.

| | |
|---|---|
| group | holding company |
| parent company | conglomerate |
| subsidiary | joint venture |
| multinational | consortium |

A **group** is a number of subsidiary companies operating under one leading company known as the **parent company**. A **subsidiary** is a company that is half or wholly owned by another company (the parent company).

A large corporation operating in many countries is called a **multinational**; most of the world's largest corporations are multinationals. A **holding company** is the leading company in a group. It holds all, or more than half of, the shares in one or more other companies. The term **conglomerate** refers to a group of companies operating in business activities which are not related to that of the leading company in the group.

When two or more companies come together to work on a particular project, or to form another company, they form a **joint venture**. In such cases, the two companies involved remain separate legal entities. A **consortium** is a group of companies which come together to undertake a project which any one of the members cannot carry out alone.

*The **group's** shares fell by 11 per cent because of a fall in the domestic market.*

*Our **parent company** has its headquarters in South Korea.*

*Nestlé Corporation, with its many branches and **subsidiaries**, is one of the world's largest food manufacturers.*

***Multinational** corporations now operate in every sector of industry.*

*Philip Morris is a **holding company** which owns several major American companies in the tobacco and food industries.*

*Warner Bros. is an entertainment **conglomerate** that produces television programmes, movies, home videos and comics.*

*Japanese and US firms in the textile industry continue to enter into **joint ventures** in China.*

*The hotel was finally rescued by a **consortium** of local business owners.*

> ⓘ A **branch** is a local office or shop that is part of a larger organization:
> *The largest bank in the country plans to close twenty of its branches*
> ○ **Giant** is sometimes used to talk about very large corporations:
> *Computer giant, Microsoft, is in the news this week.*

## Corporate restructuring

In the world of business, it is usual to see news of changes to the structure of companies and groups of companies. Many companies join with or buy other companies in order to have better control of a particular market, or to diversify their business. As the resulting mergers and acquisitions have many effects, for example on share prices and employment, the business community watches them with interest.

| | |
|---|---|
| merge | takeover |
| merger | hostile takeover |
| acquire a business | friendly takeover |
| make an acquisition | make a bid for something |
| take over | buyout |

When companies **merge**, they combine to form one company in an agreement known as a **merger**.

To buy another company or to win a controlling share of a company is to **acquire** a business, **make an acquisition** or **take over** a company. There are different kinds of **takeover**: a **hostile takeover** is a situation in which a company is bought out, but where the owners do not want to sell. A **friendly takeover**, on the other hand, refers to a situation in which a company is willingly bought out. When someone wants to buy a company they have to **make a bid for** it, ie. offer to buy it at a certain price.

A **buyout** is the purchase of a company, especially by its management or staff.

*Many European banks have* ***merged*** *in the last few years.*
*Talks of a* ***merger*** *between Daimler and Chrysler caused speculation about job security.*
*Nestlé Corporation* ***acquired*** *the Carnation Company in 1984.*
***Making an acquisition*** *in the software industry will greatly improve the company's future.*
*Bendix Corporation was* ***taken over*** *by Allied Corporation in 1982.*
*Rumours of a* ***takeover*** *led to a sharp rise in the company's share price.*
*The company has launched a bid for a* ***hostile takeover*** *of its main rival in the sector.*
*As a result of the* ***friendly takeover*** *of Western Foods Ltd., we can report a substantial increase in earnings.*
*Olivetti* ***makes a bid*** *for Telecom Italia.*
*As a result of a* ***management buyout (MBO)****, the footwear manufacturing business was rescued.*

# Organizational structure

The structure of organizations varies greatly according to the nature of the business. There are several factors which influence this structure, including:

- the number of locations and employees
- the economic sector
- the type of market in which they operate
- the type of customer
- the degree of management control required
- the complexity of the business activities.

Some corporations will, therefore, have many levels of management, while others may have a flatter structure with fewer layers. In recent years, the trend has been towards reducing the number of layers in large corporations.

Listed below are the terms used to describe the basic layers of management in a public limited company in the UK and a listed company in the US.

## *UK structure*

Board of Directors

⇓

Chairman of the Board

⇓

Managing Director (MD)

⇓

Deputy Managing Director

⇓

General Manager

⇓

Departmental Manager

## *US structure*

Board of Directors

⇓

President

⇓

Vice President and Chief Executive Officer (CEO)

⇓

Senior Vice President

⇓

Director

⇓

Manager

> ⓘ A director in the US is at the same level of management as a manager in the UK.

## What do companies do?

The nature of a business will determine how you describe its activities. The three phrases below are commonly used to describe a company's participation in business:

| | |
|---|---|
| **be engaged in** | **be involved in** |
| **have interests in** | |

### be engaged in (something)

*In addition to producing petroleum, the company is engaged in refining, marketing and shipping.*

### have interests in (something)

*Since the late 1980s the firm has had major interests in plastics and engineering.*

### be involved in (something)

*In the 1980s the company was involved in leisure and holiday activities, before expanding into air travel.*

## The activities of a company

A company may be involved in a wide range of activities. Below are some verbs commonly used to talk about some of them:

### *Production*

| | |
|---|---|
| produce | extract |
| manufacture | exploit |
| explore | process |
| build | |

**produce (something)**
to make or grow something: *The brewery produces a variety of light and dark beers.*

**manufacture (something)**
to make goods, eg. cars, electronics, carpets and footwear, from raw materials: *Since 1995 the firm has been manufacturing toys for the US market.*

**explore (something)**
to investigate or examine something: *In the next ten years the company will explore the uses of alternative energy sources.*

**build (something)**
to construct something: *Until the 1980s, Honda vehicles were designed and built in Japan for sale around the world.*

**extract (something)**
to obtain something, eg. minerals, through a process such as mechanical separation: *As well as extracting it, the corporation processes and markets the petroleum.*

**exploit (something)**
to make the best use of something, eg. resources: *Large oil producers such as Exxon exploit the natural resources of the planet.*

**process (something)**
to change raw materials into a new product by using machines, chemicals etc.: *The fish are then processed and used to make a variety of products.*

## *Operations*

| | | |
|---|---|---|
| operate | sell | offer |
| buy | provide | import |
| purchase | supply | export |

**operate**
to do business: *We will continue to operate out of Singapore, though our manufacturing plant will be relocated to Thailand.*

**purchase (something)**
to buy something: *The decision was made to purchase components in Mexico and transport them to the US for assembly.*

**sell (something)**
to give something in exchange for money: *Guinness is sold in over 120 countries.*

**provide (something)**
to give or supply something: *Their hotels provide good service at an affordable price.*

**supply (something)**
to give or provide goods or services: *Can you supply us with paper for the next six months?*

**offer (something)**
to put something forward for acceptance or rejection: *The range of services we offer is unmatched by our competitors in the industry.*

**import (something)**
to buy something and bring it into another country: *Seventy-five per cent of the goods we import come from South America.*

**export (something)**
to send goods, services and ideas to another country: *We export luxury items to Canada and Northern Europe.*

## *Finance*

| | |
|---|---|
| invest | finance |

**invest (in something)**
to put money into something (eg. shares or property) in order to

make money (see chapter 11): *The company has invested heavily in its Asian subsidiary companies.*

**finance (something)**
to obtain or supply money for something: *As a venture capital company we finance other businesses.*

## A company profile

Metcalf plc, the multinational manufacturer of food products, is based in Liverpool, UK, and operates factories, sales offices and depots in over sixty countries. Metcalf's chief products are chocolate snacks, canned fruit and vegetables, ice cream, soups and teas.

The company was established in 1898 as a small English business producing chocolate. This would later form the core of Metcalf. In the twenties, Metcalf diversified and added canned goods to its product range, and by 1930 the company had greatly expanded its business throughout the UK and northern Europe.

1985 saw a merger with BTL Foods in Michigan, USA, and the new Metcalf was floated on the Stock Exchange ten years later. Metcalf plc has recently acquired a Japanese confectionery manufacturer, and continues its expansion plans.

In addition to food production, Metcalf has interests in pharmaceuticals, plastics and leisure activities.

# 2

# Meetings

Most managers spend many hours in meetings, which play an essential role in the life of an organization. An effective business meeting has a clear purpose, a list of points to discuss, a result, and finally, a report of what took place at the meeting. It should take as short a time as possible.

There are many different types of meeting, and in the workplace you may be involved in some of the following: board meetings, departmental meetings, team meetings, staff meetings, weekly meetings and, the most formal of all, annual general meetings.

## Reasons for meetings

Meetings may be held in order to satisfy a company's legal obligations. A meeting held for this reason might be an annual general meeting (AGM) for a limited company. Here are some other reasons why meetings take place in an organization, with some specific examples.

**decision-making**
*selecting a candidate for a job*
*buying new equipment*

**information-gathering**
*reporting on a conference*
*market research*

**idea-generating**
*sales strategy*
*product development*

**reviewing/evaluating**
*staff appraisal*
*year-end review*

**problem-solving**
*late delivery of supplies*
*shortage of skilled workers*

**information-giving**
*training*
*presenting results*

**negotiating**
*suppliers' contracts*
*pay and conditions*

## Word partnerships: a meeting

The following verbs are commonly used before 'a meeting':

| | |
|---|---|
| arrange<br>organize<br>schedule<br>call<br>run<br>chair<br>have<br>hold<br>attend<br>participate in<br>go to<br>be present at<br>postpone<br>cancel | ... a meeting |

*We've **arranged** a sales meeting for Friday at two o'clock.*
*Terry, can you **organize** a meeting with the sales representatives for Tuesday or Wednesday?*
*Patrick, can we **schedule** a review meeting for next week?*
*I have **called** this emergency meeting to address the product recall.*
*We can't **have** the meeting today, so it will **be held** next week instead.*
*Can you tell me how many people are expected to **attend** the planning meeting?*
*We would have better results if more people **participated in** the meetings.*
*Sorry, I can't **go to** the team meeting tomorrow. I'm going to Paris.*
*The Managing Director **was present at** the meeting but he said very little.*
*Mariko, can you **run** the meeting on Thursday?*
*Josep Gil, our partner from Barcelona, will **chair** this month's meeting.*
*We've had to **postpone** two meetings this week because of illness. They've been rearranged for next week.*
*Mr Gallagher has been called away so we've had to **cancel** the marketing meeting.*

# Key words: the formal meeting

| | |
|---|---|
| agenda | AGM |
| minutes | EGM |
| chair | AOB |
| secretary | vote |
| participants | |

**agenda**
a list of items to be discussed at a meeting: *If you would like any items included on the agenda, please let me know before one o'clock on Wednesday.*

**minutes (*plural*)**
an official record of the proceedings of a meeting: *A copy of the minutes has been sent to everybody concerned.*

**chair**
the person who controls a meeting, also known as chairman, chairwoman or chairperson: *A new chair has been appointed.*

**secretary**
the person who is responsible for the agenda and the minutes of a meeting: *Contact the secretary if you can't attend the meeting.*

**participants**
the people who attend a meeting: *How many participants are we expecting?*

**AGM**
annual general meeting; a meeting of directors and shareholders of a company which is held once a year: *The AGM of Lincoln plc will be held at Leeds International Centre on Tuesday, 27 April 1999 at 11.00.*

**EGM**
extraordinary general meeting; a special meeting of directors and shareholders to discuss an urgent matter: *An extraordinary general meeting was called to discuss the company's merger.*

**AOB**
any other business; an item on an agenda which gives participants an opportunity to raise points that were not already included in the agenda: *Thank you George. Now, is there any other business?*

**vote**
an expression of opinion or preferences about a question, for example, the choice of a candidate: *Each shareholder at the AGM has a vote.*

> ⓘ The term **secretary** can refer to any of three different positions:
> - **company secretary**: a senior position in a company; the job-holder is often on the Board of Directors.
> - **secretary**: 1. the job title of someone whose work involves supporting another person or a department with correspondence, appointments and administrative work.
> - **secretary**: 2. a specific role in a meeting or an official position on a committee.

## *Example of an agenda*

**Agenda**

**Training Development Programme**

**Date: 17 July 2000**

Time: 11.30

Place: Room 202

1. Apologies
2. Minutes of last meeting
3. Matters arising
4. Report on Sept–Feb training programme
5. Proposed changes
6. Final arrangements for April–Oct programme
7 AOB
8. Date of next meeting

**apologies (for absence)**: announcement of names of people who cannot attend

**matters arising**: topics that need to be discussed or reported related to the minutes of the last meeting

## The chair

The **chair** or **chairperson** is the leader of a meeting — the person who controls the direction that it takes. He or she is responsible for the following:

- introducing the agenda
- introducing the speakers, if appropriate
- running the meeting
- ensuring that rules are followed
- encouraging everybody to take part
- preventing digressions
- timekeeping
- achieving objectives of the meeting
- summing up at the end
- setting the date of the next meeting if necessary

> ⓘ The terms **chairperson** and **chair** are preferable to *chairman* or *chairwoman*, which are often considered to be sexist.

## Essential language of meetings

### *Opening*

The phrases below can be used to help you to structure and run a meeting effectively in English.

**Starting the meeting**
Good morning, everyone. I think we should make a start.
Right, shall we begin?
OK, can we start now please?
We have received apologies from [names of people who cannot attend].

**Introducing the participants, when necessary**
I'd like to introduce our partners from Peru and Chile.

**Purpose of the meeting**
We are here to discuss (the recent changes in our production methods).

The purpose of this meeting is to (plan the June conference).
What we want to do today is (come to a decision about staffing levels).

### Introducing the agenda

Does everybody have a copy of the agenda?
You will see that there are (four) points on the agenda.

### The minutes of the previous meeting (if relevant)

Can we take the minutes as read? [*this means 'Does everybody accept that the minutes are accurate?'*]
Proposed? [*someone indicates that they will propose this by raising their hand*]
Seconded? [*a second person does the same to confirm the proposal*]

### First point

Now, I'd like to move on to the first point.
The first point on the agenda is (Paul's proposals to improve our website).

### Asking for contributions

Who would like to start?
I'd like to ask Mr Wheeler to tell us (his views on the subject).
Can we hear from Human Resources on that please?
Mrs Bates, would you like to comment on that?

### Handing over to another person

Now, over to you James.
Mr Reid, would you like to take it from here?

### Bringing others in

Pamela, how do you feel about what Jerry's said?
George, have you got any comments on that?
Would you like to add anything, Martha?

### Controlling the speakers

Sorry Rob, I'll have to stop you there.
Mike, can you let Paula finish?
We are moving away from the point here.
Can you be brief?

### Timekeeping

Right, that leaves us with about twenty minutes to discuss (the final point).

We need to move on now if we are going to get through everything.

### Summarizing key points during the meeting

The main points we have looked at are (how the tax changes will affect the company, and what we can do about these changes).

So the issues we've looked at so far are (shipping costs and delivery times).

## *Discussion*

The following phrases are designed to help you to take part in the discussion during a meeting.

### Asking for opinions

What do you think, Rob?

Could we hear what Rowan has to say?

What's your view on this?

### Giving opinions

I feel (it would be too expensive).

I think (Jack's right).

It seems to me that (there are two questions here).

It is clear that (profits are down).

In my view (this merger is not going to benefit the company).

### Agreeing

I agree.

I agree with (John).
(what John said).

That's right!

Absolutely!

Can we agree on this point?

### Disagreeing

I don't agree

I'm sorry. I can't agree with that.

I'm afraid I completely disagree with you.

That can't be right!

### Interrupting

Excuse me, can I just say a word?

Sorry to interrupt but (that's not the way I see the situation).

### Handling interruptions

Could you just let me finish?

I'll come to that later.
Yes, go ahead please.

**Indicating that you are listening**

Yes, I see.
Right.
Mm, I understand.

**Asking for clarification**

Sorry, I didn't catch what you said.
What exactly do you mean?
Are you saying that (the statistics are wrong)?
Could you just go over that last part again?

**Referring to other speakers**

As Pat said, (we have to deal with the problem now).
Going back to what Connor was saying, (we seem to have little choice).

## *Ending*

The chairperson should close the meeting by summarizing any decisions that have been taken, as well as outlining any follow-up action that will happen as a result of the meeting.

Here are some phrases to help with this:

**Summing up**

Now, to summarize what's been said, (the US suppliers can no longer provide what we need).
So, we've agreed to (put the decision to the workforce).
The decisions taken here today are (firstly, to increase the advertising budget by ten per cent, secondly to ...).

**Summarizing follow-up action**

Paul will look into (the cost of hiring equipment).
Before the next meeting we need to (carry out market research).
Carol, can you follow up the (problem in the canteen)?
So, who's going to (contact Head Office about this)?

**Closing the meeting**

That's all for today.
Let's finish there.
Thank you for coming.

**Arranging next meeting (if appropriate)**
The next meeting will be on [date, time].
I'll be in touch about the date of the next meeting.
What day would suit people for the next meeting? Can you check your diaries?

## The minutes

Minutes should be written as soon as possible after the meeting, and circulated to the participants and others who were unable to attend. The minutes of a meeting are written in an impersonal style, reporting what was said by whom, decisions made, action to be taken, conflicts, and so on.

### Minutes of meeting held on 17 July 2000

**Present:** Joanne McGarrigle, Marie Eagleton, Bob Newman, Ana Maria Tejos, Steve Vandersteen, Diane Moore, Richard Mills, Denis O'Leary

1. **Apologies**
   Apologies were received from Jean Thornton and Will Pidgeon
2. **Minutes**
   The minutes of the meeting held on 6 June were approved and were accepted as a true record.
3. **Matters Arising**
   BN reported that the business graduates had been notified about the dates of the project presentations.

   DM thanked the Human Resources Department for their reports, all of which have been received.

   Still awaiting confirmation of the Wright Rooms for September seminars.
4. **Reports**
   The reports were distributed. SV suggested that each should be summarized. The chair stated that in view of the absence of JT and WP, this should not be done at this meeting. Following discussion it was decided that this could be done informally outside the meeting if anyone needed information that was not included in the reports.
5. …

# 3

# Negotiations

Negotiating is the process of trying to reach an agreement, or to decide something through discussion. People negotiate in a variety of situations, from shopping in a market to taking part in United Nations peace talks. The world of business provides many opportunities for negotiating:

- An employee and employer may negotiate working conditions, eg. a pay rise, a company car, a travel allowance.
- Sales staff and customers negotiate the price of a sale, the terms of payment, delivery dates, discounts and product specifications.
- A company will negotiate a contract with a distributor.
- Two groups will try to reach agreement over the sale of a business.
- Unions have talks with management over members' pay and working conditions.

While some negotiations take place over a series of formal meetings, others may be carried out in a five-minute telephone conversation.

The aim of a negotiation is to reach agreement or resolve differences. The skills you need and the language you use will be similar in any type of negotiation. This chapter looks at these skills, as well as key words and useful phrases, to help you in your negotiations.

## Key words and phrases

### *People*

This section tells you about words used to talk about the people who negotiate, especially in a formal situation.

| | |
|---|---|
| **negotiator** | **opposite number** |
| **representative** | **counterpart** |

**negotiator**
a person who negotiates: *He's a very* | *experienced* | *skilful* | *tough* | *successful* | *negotiator.*

**representative**
a person who acts and speaks for his or her organization: *Our accountant will be our representative in this discussion.*

**opposite number**
the person you are dealing with in a negotiation: *Have you met your opposite number yet?*

**counterpart**
a person of equal status in another organization: *The financial controller contacted his counterpart in a rival company.*

## *During a negotiation*

Below are some phrases that describe what happens within the negotiation process.

| | |
|---|---|
| **enter into negotiations (with someone)** | **compromise over** |
| **sit round the negotiating table** | **settle differences** |
| **bargain** | **iron out problems or differences** |
| **haggle over** | **propose (something)** |
| **make concessions** | **common ground** |

**enter into negotiations (with someone)**
to start discussions with someone: *We are hoping to enter into negotiations with our main competitors.*

**sit round the negotiating table**
to come together in a meeting: *I think it's time to sit round the negotiating table and discuss our differences.*

**bargain**
to discuss or argue about something in order to try to find agreement: *After bargaining for hours, they finally agreed on a price.*

**haggle over (something)**
to argue about the price of an item before buying or selling: *Do you think the deal is worth haggling over?*

**make concessions**
to give up or grant something, especially after discussion: *We are prepared to make concessions on price, but not on delivery dates.*

**compromise (over an issue)**
to reach agreement by modifying aims and objectives: *Both partners were ready to compromise over the amount of share capital needed.*

**settle differences**
to come to an agreement over points of difference: *Lawyers were called in to settle the remaining differences.*

**iron out problems or differences**
to settle something through discussion: *I feel that with a little effort our differences can be ironed out.*

**propose (something)**
to make a suggestion: *Mr Ferreira, would you like to propose some changes to the plans?*

**common ground**
a shared basis for agreement: *The two groups need to build on common ground before continuing their discussions.*

## *Concluding the negotiation*

You hope to reach agreement in the final stages of a negotiation, though this may not happen every time. Here are some phrases to describe what happens at the end of the negotiation process.

| | |
|---|---|
| **agree to (something)** | **draw up an agreement** |
| **agree with (someone or something)** | **a win-win situation** |
| | **break down** |
| **agree on (a point)** | **pull out of (eg. an arrangement)** |

**agree to (something)**
to accept eg. an offer: *I'm afraid we cannot agree to the terms you have offered.*

**agree with (someone)**
to have the same opinion as someone: *Perhaps you agree with me?*

**agree on (a point)**
to come to an agreement: *Although we agreed on the price, we were not able to agree on the payment period.*

**draw up an agreement**
to prepare a written document showing the terms of agreement: *The agreement will be drawn up and signed at our next meeting.*

**a win-win situation**
a situation where both sides are satisfied: *It seems to me that we should be able to achieve a win-win situation.*

**break down**
to fail and come to an end: *Talks to resolve the dispute have broken down.*

**pull out of (eg. an arrangement)**
to withdraw from something such as a meeting, discussion or negotiation: *ERC Inc have pulled out of joint venture talks.*

## Skills

In a negotiation, as in all business situations, it is an advantage to be well prepared. Below are some ideas to help you prepare for your negotiations.

### *Before the negotiation*

- Be clear about your aims and objectives.
- Aim for a win-win situation.
- Decide on your targets; the maximum you hope to achieve and the minimum you are willing to accept.
- Be prepared to compromise.
- Plan your bargaining strategy; make a list of your aims and decide where you can make concessions and where you cannot.
- Know your weaknesses as well as your strengths.
- Be ready to make proposals.
- Think about how the other side will respond to your proposals.
- Be clear about your role if you are part of a team.

### *During the negotiation*

- Try to build on common ground.
- Suggest realistic alternatives if your proposals are rejected.

- Support your arguments with figures and calculations.
- Stay calm.
- Listen.
- Confirm what is being agreed during the negotiation.
- Try to understand the other side's point of view if you are dealing with conflict.
- Be aware of the culture of the people you are talking to. Their way of doing things may be very different to yours.

## Essential language of negotiations

Below is a list of common phrases used in negotiations:

### *Starting the negotiation*

#### Welcoming

Welcome to [company name].
It's good to have you with us today.
It's nice to see you again.

#### General conversation

I hope you had a good trip.
Did you have any problems getting here?

#### Opening negotiations

We see this as an opportunity for us to discuss (our common aims).
May I suggest that we begin by (asking Paul to show us his samples)?
Shall we get down to business?
Today we are | planning to (discuss the opening of the centre).
| going to (deal with two essential points).
| hoping to (reach a consensus).

#### Stating aims and objectives

We would like to clarify our position on (the parking facilities).
Firstly I'd like to state our objectives for this meeting. (We would like to come to an agreement about hourly pay and contracts for casual workers.)
There are two questions I would like to discuss here today. (Firstly, the estimated cost of the building, and secondly, the time-frame.)
May I give you an outline of what we hope to do today?

## *Negotiating*

### Exploring positions

Can I just clarify how you feel (about the proposal)?
What do think of (the idea)?
Could you explain your position on this?
Can I just ask you (to explain your position on this point)?
Can you give me an idea of (what you are willing to offer)?

### Bargaining

We can offer (a very competitive deal).
Would you be willing to (look at the figures again)?
We are willing to consider (your offer of forty million).
The problem here seems to be (the discount).
That would be fine so long as (you agree to our delivery dates).
What would you say if (we were to offer you a two-year warranty)?

### Inviting proposals

What would your proposal be?
Would you like to suggest something?
What do you suggest?

### Making proposals

I'd like to start by suggesting (that we look at our accountant's figures).
Our proposal would be to (open the centre in July 2001).
I propose that we should (consider the number of units first).
I'd like to suggest (a six-month trial period).

### Reacting to proposals

I see what you mean.
I take your point but (that's not a long term view).
That may be so. However, (it's not what we agreed in our last meeting).

### Making concessions

We are willing to (compromise on price) if you can (guarantee the quality).
We could accept this provided that (it is carried out immediately).
I could agree to (talk to our suppliers) if you (are willing to hold your decision).
Would you be interested in (talking to our surveyors)?

### Asking for clarification

Does that mean (you accept a price of $30 per box)?
When you say (soon) do you mean (within the next two weeks)?
Can I ask you to go over that again?
Are you saying that (you can supply us)?
So if I understand you correctly, you're saying (it's too expensive).

### Suggesting alternatives

How about (trying the dealer on Maple Road)?
We could also (wait for the market research results).
Shall we look at our options?
It seems to me that there are other ways to approach this.
Alternatively, we could (look for a local supplier).

## *Concluding the negotiation*

### Showing agreement

Yes, I think we can agree on that.
That's acceptable to us.
Fine!
It's a deal!

### Rejecting proposals

We could not accept (those conditions).

| | | |
|---|---|---|
| That would be | very difficult | for us. |
| | impossible. | |

### Summarizing

Now I'd like to summarize the main points of our discussion.
So, to summarize our proposals, (we offer a price of £400 per unit, delivery in six months).

### Confirming agreement

I'd like to check what we've agreed.
I think we should run through what's been decided so far.

### Looking to the future

Our next step will be to (order the parts).
I hope we can meet again to (finalize the agreement).
A formal contract will be drawn up before our next meeting.

### Ending (after a successful negotiation)

Thank you for coming.
It's been a pleasure doing business with you.

**Breaking off unsuccessful negotiations**
I'm afraid we are not going to agree on this.
I see no point in continuing this discussion.

> ⓘ Use of **I** or **we**: If you are negotiating as an individual you will need to use **I** in your discussions. If you are representing a company you may prefer to use **we** to show that you have the strength of the company behind you.

## Useful language

In a negotiation you may need to argue firmly to achieve what you want, and to do this effectively you need to emphasize important points, and support your arguments with additional information.

### *Emphasizing*

Using intensifiers such as adverbs:

**Subject + adverb + verb**

| | |
|---|---|
| really | *I **really** can't agree with what you have just suggested.* |
| completely | *We **completely** reject the last proposal.* |
| strongly | *I **strongly** recommend that we wait for the report.* |
| totally | *I **totally** oppose the building of a chemical plant in this area.* |
| deeply | *We **deeply** regret the number of redundancies.* |
| firmly | *We **firmly** believe that our partnership will survive.* |
| honestly | *I **honestly** feel that we can create more jobs.* |

**Subject + verb 'to be' + adverb + adjective**

| | |
|---|---|
| really | *This prospect is **really** exciting for the company.* |
| extremely | *We are **extremely** pleased with its performance.* |
| highly | *It is **highly** unlikely that we will sell.* |
| absolutely | *It's **absolutely** imperative that the employees are with us on this.* |

## *Making an additional point*

| | |
|---|---|
| what's more | *It's excellent quality, and **what's more**, it's economical.* |
| also | *Well, we can produce cheaply and **also** on time.* |
| plus | *Our goods are locally made. **Plus**, they're good value.* |
| in addition | *My performance is excellent. **In addition** I am highly motivated.* |

# 4

# Presentations

A presentation is a prepared talk about a particular subject. There are many kinds of presentation: formal and informal; long or short; presenting a product or company or organization; to a known audience or a group of strangers; to a group with little or no knowledge of the subject or to a group with expert knowledge.

A presentation may be given to train people, to stimulate interest in a subject, to provoke discussion or argument, to gain support, or simply to give information.

For any presentation, there are some skills that will help you to perform more effectively. This chapter will look at these skills, and focus in particular on the key words and phrases that will help you to make effective presentations in English.

## Key words

### *General*

| | |
|---|---|
| audience | speaker |
| conference | speech |
| meeting | talk |
| presentation | |

**audience**
a group of people listening to and watching a speaker or performer: *How many people do we expect in today's audience?*

**conference**
a series of meetings and presentations, often where representatives of a particular industry or profession meet for several days: *The sales conference will be held in Sydney this year.*

**meeting**
an occasion when people get together to discuss something or make decisions: *The weekly planning meeting has been cancelled.*

**presentation**
a prepared talk given to an audience: *She has been invited to give a presentation at the board meeting.*

**speaker**
a person who gives a presentation: *One of the speakers is an expert in company law.*

**speech**
a formal talk, often given by politicians: *The minister's speech lasted for over an hour.*

**talk**
another word for presentation: *I'd like to thank our speaker for a very interesting talk.*

## *Equipment and visual aids*

To help the audience follow your presentation it is a good idea to use some of the equipment and visual aids listed below to display your pictures, charts, graphs or diagrams.

**computer graphics**
**diapositive (*AmE*)**
**slide (*BrE*)**
**flipchart**
**glossary**
**handout**
**OHP**
**sample**
**slide projector**
**transparency**
**whiteboard**

**computer graphics**
images and text stored on computer which can be projected directly onto a screen.

**slide (*BrE*) diapositive (*AmE*)**
a small piece of photographic film showing images or text, used with a slide projector.

**flipchart**
large sheets of paper on a stand.

**glossary**
a list of words or terms, with definitions.

**handout**
a page or pages distributed among the audience showing information related to a talk, such as the outline, important data or diagrams.

**OHP**
overhead projector; a machine which projects images and text from a transparency onto a screen.

**sample**
a small amount of a product for showing to people as an example.

**slide projector**
a machine which projects photographic images onto a screen.

**transparency (*BrE*) slide (*AmE*)**
a sheet of clear plastic showing images or text which are projected onto a screen by an overhead projector.

**whiteboard**
a large white board for writing on, common in classrooms and offices.

## Presentation skills

An effective speaker is well prepared, enthusiastic, and communicates easily with the audience. A successful presentation needs to be well planned. Below are some ideas that may assist in the process of preparing and giving a presentation.

### *Preparing a presentation*

- Know your subject well in order to deliver your talk confidently.
- Use brief notes or cards to refer to during your talk, rather than reading from a long written text.
- Give your talk a clear, logical structure with an introduction, main points which are linked, and a conclusion.
- Be realistic about the amount of information you can include in your talk, and support your main points with examples and other relevant details.
- Think about your audience and their knowledge of the subject. Try to anticipate the kind of questions they may ask.
- Check how long your talk will take by practising beforehand.

- ❍ Practise with the equipment you are going to use, if possible.
- ❍ Make your visual aids clear and easy to understand. They should be visible from every part of the room.
- ❍ Check your visual aids and handouts for spelling and grammar mistakes.
- ❍ Practise the pronunciation of unfamiliar words before your talk. Check in a dictionary or ask someone who speaks English well to help you.

### *Giving a presentation*

- ❍ Face the audience. Make as much eye contact as possible.
- ❍ Tell the audience what you are going to do. (See **Essential language of presentations** below.)
- ❍ Keep your language simple; avoid complex sentences.
- ❍ Speak slowly and remember to pause from time to time.
- ❍ Have a drink of water near you during the talk.
- ❍ Enjoy yourself!

## How to structure a presentation

A good presentation has a structure that is clear to both the speaker and the audience. Here is a simple model to help you organize your ideas.

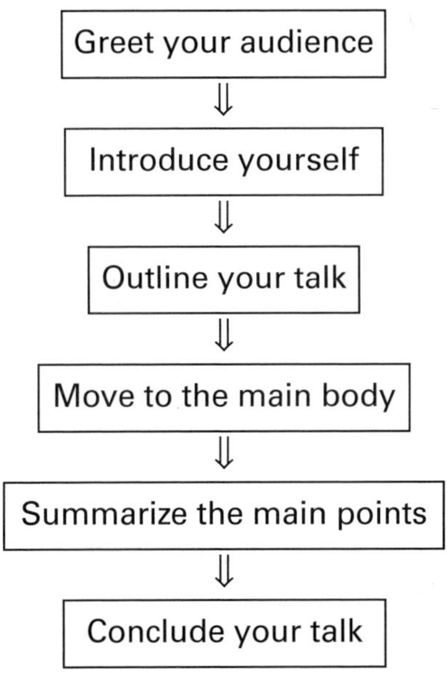

⇓

| Invite questions from the audience |
|---|

⇓

| Accept questions and comments |
|---|

## Essential language of presentations

It is helpful for an audience if the presenter guides them through the structure of a talk. Below is a list of expressions which can be used to signal the different stages of a presentation.

At the end of the first section there is an example of how to start a presentation.

### *The Introduction*

#### Greeting the audience

Good | morning
| afternoon
| evening

Good evening ladies and gentlemen
Hello everybody.
I was very happy to be invited to speak to you today.
It's very nice to be here.
I'm very pleased to be with you.
It's a pleasure to be here today.

#### Introducing yourself

My name's [your name] and I'm from [company name].
I am the [your job] at [company name].
I am [your name] and I represent [company name].
I think you all know me. [*if giving a talk to colleagues, for example*]

#### Explaining the purpose of your talk

I'm here today to talk to you about [the subject of your talk].
I've come here today to | explain (the sales targets for the next six months).
| look at (the role of the dealer in our organization).
| describe (successful marketing strategies).

I'd like to talk to you about (investments).

### Outlining the structure of the talk

I've divided my talk into four parts.
My talk will focus on three main areas.
I plan to talk about the history, the present situation and the future development of (the coffee industry).
In the first part I will look at (the background).
The second part will deal with (the consumers' perception of the product).
In the final part I'll show you (the new sales figures).

### Saying how long your talk will take

My talk will take about forty minutes.
I plan to speak for about thirty minutes.

### Saying when you prefer to answer questions

I'll be happy to answer your questions at the end of my talk.
Please feel free to interrupt me during my talk if you have a question.

In the following passage, Marina Potter, Marketing Manager at Arcon plc, is giving a talk to a group of students about marketing:

## Presentation

Good evening ladies and gentlemen. I'm very pleased to be with you today. My name's Marina Potter. I am the Marketing Manager at Arcon plc. I'd like to talk to you about 'the marketing environment'.

I've divided my talk into three parts. In the first part I'll look at political and legal forces. The second part will deal with economic and competitive forces, and in the final part I'll show you how technological forces have made an impact on our marketing activities.

I plan to speak for about thirty minutes. I'll be happy to answer your questions at the end of my presentation.

I'd like to start now by looking at the meaning of the term 'marketing environment' ...

## *The main body*

### Moving to the first point

I'd like to start now by looking at (the figures for 1999).
In this first part of my talk I want to look at (the profit and loss account).
Firstly, I'd like to consider (the question of data protection).
To begin with, I'm going to review (recent developments in technology).

### Ending a point

Right, that's all I have to say about (Russia).

### Moving to a new point

Moving on now to my next point: (share performance).
Now I'd like to look at (the role of the Sales Manager).
Let's turn now to (international trade).

### Describing a sequence

Firstly, (we proposed changes to the packaging).
First of all, (we decided to analyse the competition).
Secondly, (we examined potential markets in the Middle East).
Then (we looked at the figures for the last five years).
Next, (the decision was made to cut spending on product development).
After that, (we checked the results).
Finally, (we showed that the market could be turned around in 18 months).

### Talking about a previous point

In the introduction I said (I was going to talk about pricing policy).
In the first part of my talk I mentioned (the importance of equal opportunities).
As I've already said, (tradition is a relevant factor).
Remember what I talked about a moment ago? Now I'd like to (expand on that).

### Talking about a future point or piece of information

I'll go into this in more detail at a later stage.
I'll come to that later.

### Introducing a visual aid

Could you please look at the screen for a moment?
As you can see in the diagram, (there's been a steady rise in profits).
I'd like to show you an example of what I mean.
Have a look at (the diagram on the left).
Take a look at (this).

### Getting back to a main idea

Let me return to what I was saying before.
To get back to my main point: (rates of expansion).
As I was saying, (we need to look at the drawbacks).

### Involving the audience

As you are aware, (the bid was abandoned).
As you know, (the trade gap has narrowed).
You may be aware of (the fall in property prices this month).

| | |
|---|---|
| Can anybody suggest a | figure? |
| | reason? |
| | solution? |

### Handling interruptions

That's an interesting question. I'll come to that at the end.
If I could just answer that later.
Yes, thank you, I was just coming to that.

### Summarizing

So, what we have looked at here today is (the outlook for the industry over the next five years).
I'd like to end now by summarizing the main points of my talk.

## *Conclusion*

### Concluding

That's all I have to say about this subject for now.
Thank you very much for your attention.
I'd like to end now by thanking you for your attention.

### Inviting questions

I'll be happy to answer your questions now.
If you have any questions I'll be pleased to answer them now.
Any questions or comments?
We have some time now for questions and comments.

## *Questions and comments*

### Handling questions

That's an interesting comment. Thank you for that.
Right, thank you for that observation.
That's an interesting question, which I'll try to answer.
I'm afraid I'm not able to answer that question.
I don't think I can answer that just now but I can try to find out for you.

# The language of trends

When giving a presentation, a speaker may use graphs and charts to explain movements and changes in, for example, economic statistics, markets, company performance, share prices, profits, costs, staff turnover, sales figures, and R&D (research and development) spending. To do this effectively, it is important to use the appropriate language.

The words below are commonly used to describe trends. They are grouped according to similarity of meaning.

## *Upward movement*

### General upward movement

| | |
|---|---|
| **go up** (*verb*) | *Profits* ***have gone up*** *by 2% in the past year.* |
| **raise** (*verb*) | *The Government* ***has raised*** *taxes for married couples.* |
| **raise** (*noun; (AmE)*) | *He was unhappy with his salary and asked for a* ***raise****.* |
| **rise** (*verb*) | *Unemployment* ***rose*** *steadily in the first quarter of the year.* |
| **rise** (*noun)* | *There's been a steady* ***rise*** *in new business over the last six months.* |
| **climb** (*verb*) | *Domestic sales* ***climbed*** *rapidly during the first quarter.* |
| **climb** (*noun*) | *A* ***climb*** *in production costs is expected in the next quarter.* |
| **increase** (*verb)* | *The number of short-term contracts will* ***increase*** *due to a change in policy.* *The management will probably* ***increase*** *staff numbers during peak periods.* |

| | |
|---|---|
| **increase** (*noun*) | *Economists predict an* ***increase*** *in inflation.* |

### Rapid upward movement

| | |
|---|---|
| **jump** (*verb*) | *Share prices* ***have jumped*** *to a record high.* |
| **jump** (*noun*) | *We can expect to see a* ***jump*** *in retail prices.* |
| **surge** (*verb*) | *Stock markets* ***surged*** *on news of interest rate cuts in the USA.* |
| **surge** (*noun*) | *Recent data shows a* ***surge*** *of interest in business courses.* |
| **soar** (*verb*) | *Unemployment in Britain* ***soared*** *to over 3 million in the 1980s.* |

## *Downward movement*

### General downward movement

| | |
|---|---|
| **go down** (*noun*) | *The $US* ***went down*** *3 cents against the Yen yesterday.* |
| **fall** (*verb*) | *Unemployment* ***fell*** *last month from 1.7 million to just below 1.6 million.* |
| **fall** (*noun*) | *International Paper Mills reported a* ***fall*** *in profits from $235 million to $188 million.* |
| **drop** (*verb*) | *Consumer spending* ***drops*** *dramatically as interest rates go up.* |
| **drop** (*noun*) | *Arcon Inc. reports a severe* ***drop*** *in profits.* |
| **decline** (*verb*) | *Traditional industries such as coal and textiles* ***have declined*** *in Europe* |
| **decline** (*noun*) | *Oil prices have seen a* ***decline*** *in recent weeks due to overproduction.* |
| **reduce** (*verb*) | *The company is planning to* ***reduce*** *the size of the workforce.* |
| **reduction** (*noun*) | *A* ***reduction*** *in the staffing budget has led to redundancies.* |
| **decrease** (*verb*) | *The price of computers is expected to* ***decrease*** *further as semiconductors become cheaper.* *Insurance companies hope to* ***decrease*** *the number of pay-outs.* |

| | |
|---|---|
| decrease (*noun*) | *Angry workers are protesting against a* ***decrease*** *in working hours.* |
| worsen (*verb*) | *The state of the environment is expected to* ***worsen*** *in the next century.* |
| downturn (*noun*) | *Asian economies have experienced a significant* ***downturn*** *in recent years.* |

## Rapid downward movement

| | |
|---|---|
| plummet (*verb*) | *Technotron shares* ***plummeted*** *yesterday on news of product failures.* |
| plunge (*verb*) | *The Nikkei Index* ***plunged*** *below 12 000 yesterday for the first time since 1984.* |
| collapse (*verb*) | *Coffee prices* ***collapsed*** *on news of a record crop in Brazil.* |

## *Highs and lows*

| | |
|---|---|
| peak (*verb*) | *Unemployment* ***peaked*** *at nineteen per cent.* |
| reach a peak (*verb*) | *Sales* ***reached a peak*** *of 14 million units in November last year.* |
| hit a low (*verb*) | *AMC shares* ***hit*** *a record* ***low*** *of 229 yesterday* |
| bottom out (*verb*) | *Exports* ***bottomed out*** *at $206,000 in February, before rising again to $340,000 in April.* |
| fluctuate (*verb*) | *The share price* ***fluctuated*** *between 234p and 426p because of instability in the market.* |

## *No change*

| | |
|---|---|
| remain stable | *The level of profits* ***has remained stable*** *in spite of the unfavourable economic climate.* |
| remain unchanged | *The company's approach to modernization* ***has remained unchanged*** *for many years.* |
| stay the same | *Staff numbers are likely to* ***stay the same*** *for the next year.* |

## *Degree of change*

To describe the degree of change, think about what is being described, and the period covered. For example, a 1% increase in inflation in one month is generally seen as a *sharp rise*, while a 1% increase in profits over one year would be described as a *slight rise*.

| | Adverbs | Adjectives | |
|---|---|---|---|
| | *slightly* | *a slight* | |
| to rise or fall | *moderately* | *moderate* | rise or fall |
| | *significantly* | *significant* | |
| | *sharply* | *sharp* | |
| | *dramatically* | *dramatic* | |

## *Example*

Look at the graph below showing sales figures for 12 months. Then read the description of the year's performance.

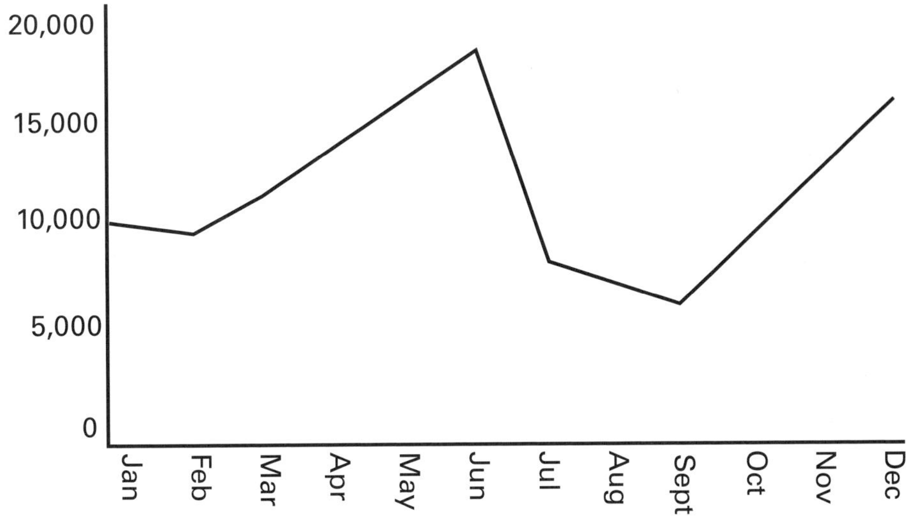


We started the year at 10,000 units. This was followed by a slight drop in February. Sales rose moderately in March to 12,000 and continued to go up sharply until June when they reached a peak of 19,000. In July sales fell dramatically to 8000 units. The situation continued to worsen in August and bottomed out at 6000 in September. Fortunately, October saw a significant increase, and by the end of the year sales had risen to 16,000.

# 5

# Telephoning

Telephoning is a very direct form of communication, and although the use of e-mail is a popular alternative, there are times when phoning someone is more effective, for example when you want to locate a particular person in an organization, or get information quickly. This chapter looks at key words, phrases and strategies that will help you with your calls.

In business, people may want to make a phone call for any of the following reasons:

- to give or get information, especially in a hurry or in an emergency
- to keep in contact with someone
- to make an appointment or to make arrangements
- to confirm details of something, such as an order
- to clarify a misunderstanding
- to make a complaint or explain a problem
- to follow up a meeting
- to thank someone

## Key expressions

The following expressions can be used to talk about telephoning. **Phone**, **call** and **ring** are other ways of saying 'telephone' (*verb*).

make a call
give someone a call/ring
call back
return someone's call
call someone back
get back to someone
put someone through
get through to someone
be engaged (*BrE*)
be busy (*AmE*)
be on the phone
hold on
hang up

**make a call**
to telephone someone: *I'll meet you downstairs in five minutes. I just have to make a call.*

**give someone a call**
an informal way of saying 'call' or 'phone': *I'll give you a call on Monday to tell you my arrival time.*

**call back**
to telephone someone again: *She's not in? I'll call back tomorrow.* ❑ *I'll call back later.*

**return someone's call**
to call someone who called you before: *Good morning Mr Hughes. My name is Carol Macfarlane. I'm returning your call.*

**call someone back**
to call someone who called you before: *Could you ask her to call me back?*

**get back to someone**
to contact someone again: *Could you get back to me with that information?*

**put someone through**
to connect the caller to another person or department: *Could you put me through to the sales department, please?*

**get through to someone**
to be able to contact and talk to someone: *Did you manage to get through to the Marketing Director?*

**be engaged (*BrE*), be busy (*AmE*)**
to be in use; the number you are calling is not available: *The number is still engaged. I can't seem to get through.* ❑ *I'm sorry, the line's busy. Would you like to call back later?*

**be on the phone**
to be using the phone: *I'm sorry, she's on the phone just now. Can you call back later?*

**hold on**
to wait: *Hold on a moment. I'll see if she's free.*

**hang up**
to end a call and put the phone down: *After waiting for thirty minutes, he hung up.*

The words below are frequently used when telephoning or talking about calls.

**extension**
an internal telephone number: *Extension 22054* [*'double two, oh five four'*], *please*

**answering service**
an electronic service which records messages for you and gives them to you later: *I left a message with his answering service.*

**answering machine**
a machine connected to the phone which records messages from callers: *If he's not there I'll leave a message on the answering machine.*

## Saying telephone numbers

We usually say telephone numbers as individual digits.

- Note '0' can be pronounced as 'oh' or 'zero'
  eg. 01234 473950: *oh one two three four; four seven three, nine five oh*
  *zero one two three four; four seven three, nine five zero*
- As you speak, note that you can separate the digits into groups with a slight pause between them.

## Strategies for making a call

Making a phone call in a foreign language can be difficult because you cannot make eye contact, show samples, or draw diagrams; you can only communicate verbally. It is therefore important to be prepared beforehand. Remember also that the person you are speaking to may not use English as their first language.

Here are some ways you can help yourself to make effective calls:

- Learn how to greet people.
- Learn how to ask for a specific person by name or job title.
- Plan what to say if that person is not available.
- Have the relevant papers with you to refer to.
- Be ready to ask people to repeat or clarify something if necessary.

- Make sure you know how to say numbers and the alphabet in English; you may need to write names, prices, dates and other details.
- Always confirm the details at the end of a call.
- Follow up the call with a fax or an e-mail to confirm arrangements or appointments, especially if you have any doubts.

## Making a call: structure

Although every telephone call is different, you can use the simple structure and the specific phrases below to help to prepare for a call.

### *Part one*

greetings

⇓

identify yourself

⇓

get the person you want to speak to

⇓

explain the purpose of the call

### *Part two*

talk about the main subject of the call *eg.* arrangements

⇓

confirm details of the conversation

### *Part three*

signal the end of the call

⇓

thank the other person

⇓

refer to future action

⇓

close the call

## Essential language of telephoning

Below is some of the basic language you need to make and receive calls, followed by some more detailed alternatives to select from.

### Making a call

Greetings
Hello.
Good morning.
Good afternoon.

### Identifying yourself

My name is [your name].
This is [your name]. [*if the person receiving the call knows your name*]
My name is [your name]. I'm calling from [your department and the name of the company]. [*if the person receiving the call doesn't know your name*]

### Asking to speak to someone

Bob Robbins, please.
Can I speak to (Bob Newman), please? [*you know the name*]
Could you put me through to the (marketing) department, please?
I'd like to speak to (Anna Bredin), please.
Could I speak to someone in charge of (customer services), please? [*you don't know the name of anyone in that department*]
Could I speak to someone about (business accounts), please?
I'd like to speak to whoever deals with (planning permits).

### Explaining the purpose of the call

I'm calling to ask you for (a copy of invoice 221/TW).
I'm calling about (the ad in today's newspaper).
I'm phoning in connection with (the March trade fair).
I'm trying to get in touch with (John Allen).
I'm trying to find out about (model T40).

### Leaving a message

Could you give Tanya a message, please?
Do you think you could give him a message, please?
Could you ask him to call me back today?

Could you tell her that (I can't make this afternoon's meeting)?

### Thanking

Thanks for your help.
Well, thank you very much.
Thank you. You've been very helpful.
Thanks a lot. [*informal*]

### Ending

I'll talk to you soon.
Well, I'll see you next week then.
Goodbye.

> ⓘ Do not say 'I am …' to identify yourself on the phone. 'I am …' is used to introduce yourself in person, or to describe your job title or profession. Instead, say 'This is …'.
>
> ❍ When you make a call, you can check that you are speaking to the right person, department or organization by asking:
>
> *'Is that* | *James O'Brate?*
> *the Customer Services department?*
> *Wilde and Langley?*

## Receiving a call

### Greeting

Hello.
Good morning.
Good afternoon.

### Identifying yourself and your organization

Kingston Clothing, Jane speaking.
Reeves and Coates.

### Offering to help

Can I help you?
How can I help you?

### Asking who the caller is

Who's calling, please?
Who shall I say is calling?
And your name, please?

### Asking the caller to wait

Just a moment, please.
Could you hold on, please?

### Connecting the caller to the right person

Right, you are through to Mr Walters.
I'm just putting you through to her now.
I'll put you through to Accounts.

### Explaining that someone is not available

I'm sorry, he's not available just now.

I'm afraid she's | out at the moment.
| on holiday this week.
| away today.
| in a meeting just now.

Sorry. I can't locate her.
She's on another line just now. Do you want to hold?

### Offering alternatives

Would you like to leave a message?
Can I give him a message?
Could you call back later?
Can you tell me what it's in connection with?
Would you like to speak to someone else from his department?

### Taking a message

Can I have your name, please?
And your number?
Could you spell your name for me, please?

### Checking information

So, that's Paula Martinez on 558 90 96 and you would like Mr Walters to call you back.

### Ending a call

Thank you for calling.
Goodbye.

## Talking about different subjects

When you reach the person you want to speak to, there are many ways in which the conversation might develop, depending on the purpose of your call. You can choose from the situations below to help you to prepare for your calls.

## *Arrangements*

In business you frequently need to make arrangements for meetings, conferences, appointments, deliveries, travel, social events and other activities.

### Making arrangements

We need to get together | to confirm (the details of the trip).
| discuss (your proposal).
| plan (our presentation).

I'd like to meet up with you to | discuss (my idea).
| look at (the samples).

Can we meet on (Tuesday at three o'clock)?
How about (tomorrow afternoon at about four)?
That would suit me fine.
Could we deliver the order on (May 14)?
Shall I make a booking for (twelve people)?

### Changing arrangements

I'm afraid (Friday) will not be possible after all.
I'm sorry but I have to | cancel (the appointment).
| postpone (the meeting).
| delay (the delivery).
| rearrange (our schedule).

There has been a problem with (the flights).
Can we meet up a little earlier than planned?

### Making a reservation

I'd like to | book the conference room for [date, time, number of people].
| reserve a flight to [place] on [date] for [number of people].

Could I make a reservation please? A table for (eight people) at (seven o'clock) on (Thursday).

### Confirming arrangements and reservations

Right, I look forward to our meeting next week.
So that's two tickets for the fourth of May at three o'clock.
So we'll see you on Friday.

## *Requests (asking people to do things)*

### Requesting information or action

Could you tell me (the order number), please?
Would you send us the details of (the offer), please?

Do you think you could ask her to contact us?
I'd like a copy of (the report please).

#### Responding to requests

Certainly, I'd be happy to.
Yes, of course.
Sure, I'll get on to it straight away.
Sorry, I'm afraid that's not possible. [*explain why not*]
Sorry, I can't help you there.

## *Details*

It is essential to be able to give and take down names, quantities, dates, prices, addresses, numbers and other details. To do this you need to know how to spell words in English and to be able to say numbers (see Appendix).

#### Asking for details

Could you give me the reference number please?
... and your address?
What exactly is it that you need?
How many crates have you ordered?

#### Give details

That's R-O-S-C-O-M-M-O-N.
Reference Number 3 4 2 Z / R
Model number 207.

#### Asking for clarification

Could you spell that for me, please?
Did you say two o'clock?
I'm sorry, I didn't catch the | last name.
| number.
| first part of the address.
| flight time.
Could you repeat that please?
I'm sorry, I don't understand. Could you speak more slowly, please?

#### Confirming details

So, that's 200 boxes of 40 at £50 per box. OK?
So that's Mr Sean Cusack from GRT International, and you want Gretta to call you. Is that right?

## *Complaints and problems*

Explaining a problem over the phone requires preparation, so before you make your call, think about what is wrong, the words that you need to describe it in detail, and the result you want from the call.

### Making a complaint

I bought a (box of stationery supplies).
I ordered some (tools) from you last week.
I'm calling to complain about our last order.
I'm not at all happy with | the service.
| your response (to my request).
The (wiring) is faulty.
I've been waiting for (my equipment) for three months.

### Explaining your problem

I can't understand the (instructions).
The (light) doesn't seem to be working properly.

### Responding to complaints and problems

Could you tell me exactly what happened?
What seems to be the problem?
Have you tried (restarting it)?
Could you send me the details in writing?

## *Listening actively*

On the phone, it is important to let the caller know that you are listening. You can do this by using the words below.

| | |
|---|---|
| **I see.** | **Right.** |
| **Yes, I understand.** | **Okay.** |

### Apologizing

I'm sorry to hear about that.
We are sorry about all the problems you have had.

### Promising

I'll check it out and call you back.
I'll get on to that right away.
I'll see what I can do, (Mr Jefferson).
You'll get a replacement this week.

## Telephone conversations

Below are two examples of telephone conversations, one where the caller leaves a message and the other where the caller gets through to someone in the right department.

### Dialogue

In the following telephone conversation, the caller knows who he wants to speak to but she is not available:

Jonathan Rankin, a supplier of fabrics, calls Laura Williams, Purchasing Manager of a clothing manufacturer, to arrange a meeting. They have done business together before.

**Receptionist**: J-Mac Clothes. Sonia speaking. Can I help you?

**Jonathan**: This is Jonathan Rankin from R&B Fabrics. Can I speak to Laura Williams, please?

**Receptionist**: Just a moment, Mr Rankin.

**Jonathan**: Thank you.

**Receptionist**: I'm sorry. She's not available just now. Can I take a message?

**Jonathan**: Yes please. Could you tell her that we've got our new range of fabrics from India and I would like to show them to her, this week if possible. Could you ask her to call me today?

**Receptionist**: So, you want her to call you about the range of Indian fabrics?

**Jonathan**: Yes, that's right.

**Receptionist**: Right, Mr Rankin, I'll give her your message.

**Jonathan**: Thanks. Bye.

**Receptionist**: Goodbye.

## Dialogue

In this telephone conversation, the caller does not have the name of the person he wants to speak to. This is his first call to this company.

**Receptionist**: Grant and Williams. How can I help you?

**Peter**: Good morning. I'd like to speak to someone about communications seminars, please.

**Receptionist**: Just a moment please. I'll put you through to Patrick Beazley.

**Peter**: Thank you.

**Patrick**: Patrick Beazley here. Can I help you?

**Peter**: Hi. My name is Peter Cohen from the Human Resources Department of Rutland Printing. We are planning a series of seminars on communications training for our sales reps and I'm looking for some information about the services you offer.

**Patrick**: Well, we go from half-day seminars on giving presentations right through to one-week courses on cross-cultural communication. And we can tailor them for your particular needs.

**Peter**: Right ... well, could you send me some information?

**Patrick**: Yes, of course. Would you like me to come along to discuss it with you?

**Peter**: Well, at this stage I'd just like to see what you are offering.

**Patrick**: Fine. Could you just give me your address?

**Peter**: It's Rutland Printing Limited, 22 Rowland Place, York YK4 4BP.

**Patrick**: Did you say twenty-two?

**Peter**: Yes, that's right.

**Patrick**: Right, I'll send that off to you today.

**Peter**: Thanks. Goodbye.

**Patrick**: Goodbye.

# 6

# Socializing and cultural issues

Social language skills enable you to talk comfortably to people about non-business topics, for example when you first meet, during meals, before meetings and when you are parting. A lot of business is done outside the boardroom, so it is important to be able to function effectively in social situations. Obviously you can't plan for every occasion, or for all the varieties of language you will encounter. However, you can do a lot to prepare yourself to be a good socializer in English. Start by looking at these two points:

- cultural diversity
- social language

## Cultural diversity

In addition to knowing the right language to use, it is also important to appreciate cultural differences when dealing with people from other countries. Here are some comments and suggestions to consider on this aspect of business communication.

When developing the social side of a business relationship you should be able to talk about your own country, and be informed about your clients' or foreign partners' countries. It is useful to have some knowledge of the following:

- political and economic background
- main religions and their influence on the state
- regional differences
- social background eg. role of women, education
- major companies
- the sector your company operates in
- conventions eg. food and drink

> ⓘ Think carefully before introducing topics which may be sensitive eg. politics, recent history, religion. This does not mean that you should never discuss these subjects, only that you should be aware of their importance in other societies. Observe, ask questions subtly, and learn.

## Initial contact

This section looks at the language you use in a variety of social situations in the world of business.

### *Arriving at a company*

If you have an appointment, go to the reception desk and explain who you are and give the name of the person you have come to see.

My name is [your name] from [company name].
I have an appointment to see [name] at [time].

The receptionist will probably respond as follows:

Please take a seat and I'll tell him you're here.
Just a moment, please. I'll call her.
Could you go to the first floor, second door on the left, please?

### *Introductions*

#### Introducing yourself

Hello. I'm [name].
Hi. My name's [name]. Nice to meet you.
Pleased to meet you.
How do you do?

> ⓘ 'How do you do?' is not a real question. The normal response is 'How do you do?'

#### Second or subsequent meeting

Nice to see you again. How are you?
... Very well, thank you. And you?
... Fine, thanks. How are you?
... Not bad, thanks.

#### Introducing a third person

This is (Des Howard).

I'd like you to meet (Carol Walker).
I'd like to introduce my | partner, Joe Salucci
colleague
friend
associate
May I introduce (Peter Adamson)?

(i) It is usual in the UK and the USA to give a firm handshake when meeting for the first time, and when saying goodbye at the end of this meeting. At subsequent business meetings it is also common for people to shake hands.

- Names can be confusing, so when you are introducing yourself, say your name clearly and help people with the pronunciation if you see that it is difficult for them. You can tell people what you would like them to call you by saying 'Please call me ...'.
- Generally speaking, it is better not to address someone by their first name unless you are invited to do so. It is more acceptable in some countries than others. For example in the US it is very common to be on first-name terms with a business associate, quite common in the UK, but not usual in most Asian countries.

## Talking about work

At conferences, dinners, and other social occasions you will need to be able to ask and answer questions. It is usual to ask about an organization's activities, what a person does, and how long someone has worked there. However, it is not usual to ask about a person's salary. Below are some useful questions and phrases.

*So, what do you do?* *I'm a | sales representative.*
*management consultant.*
*an engineer.*
*I work at (or for) IBM.*
*I work for a company that ...*
*makes electric goods.*
*exports engine parts.*
*produces textiles.*

| | |
|---|---|
| *Who do you work for?* | *A small chemical company called (Brown and Walker).*<br>*A firm of lawyers.*<br>*Hudson Brothers.*<br>*My father's firm.*<br>*I'm self-employed.* |
| *What kind of company is it?* | *We manufacture plastic products for the home.*<br>*They're tax consultants.*<br>*It's a huge paper-processing company.*<br>*It's a clothes retailers.* |
| *How many employees are there?* | *A couple of hundred.*<br>*About three thousand.*<br>*Twenty.* |
| *Where is it based?* | *In Zurich.*<br>*We have offices in Dallas and Chicago.*<br>*Just outside Birmingham.*<br>*Near Wellington.* |
| *How long have you worked there?* | *Since I graduated.*<br>*Since 1997.*<br>*For about six years.*<br>*Actually, I've just started.* |

## Invitations

If you are a guest you may be invited to meals and for drinks, and perhaps to take part in other activities such as trips to the theatre, playing golf, or visiting public buildings. If you are receiving guests you may want to invite them to do some of these things.

### Inviting

Would you like to | come out for dinner tonight?
| go to the theatre one evening this week?
| come to my house for dinner tomorrow evening?

How about meeting for a drink later?
I'm going for dinner. Would you like to join me?
I'd like to take you out for lunch tomorrow. Are you free?

### Accepting an invitation

Yes, I'd like that very much.
Yes, I'd love to. Thank you.
I'd be delighted.
That sounds great.

### Declining an invitation

I'm afraid I can't make it tonight, but thank you.
I'm sorry but [+ reason].
I'd like to but [+ reason].
Possible reasons: I have another engagement.
I have an early flight tomorrow morning.
I've got some work to do.

### Giving gifts

I've brought you something from [your own country].
This is for you. [*as you hand the gift to someone*]
I'd like you to have this. I hope you like it.

### Response

Thank you very much.
That's very kind of you. Thank you.

> ⓘ If you are invited to someone's house for a meal it is usual to take a small gift, though the type of gift varies from one country to another. In the UK, for example, you could take a bottle of wine, a box of chocolates, some flowers, or a gift from your own country. Note, however, that in some countries it is not polite to open a gift immediately, while in others it is usual. If you are aware of the customs of the country you are visiting, you will not cause offence or be offended.

## Asking for and offering assistance

When you are receiving visitors, you will need to be able to offer assistance. If your visitor is staying in a hotel you can offer to help with any language problems, with specific shopping needs, flights, hotel rooms or food and drink.

### Making offers

Can I get you a drink?
Would you like something to eat?

Do you need anything?
Is there anything you need?
If I can help in any way, please let me know.

### Responding to offers

Yes please, that would be nice. I'll have a coffee.
No thanks, I'm fine.

### Asking for assistance

Could you tell me where I can get (a good walking map)?
Can you recommend a good hotel?
I need to print something out. Can you tell me where I can do it?
I have a problem with (my reservation). Do you think you can help me?

## *Eating and drinking*

| *Offering a drink* | *Responding* |
|---|---|
| Can I get you a drink? | Yes, please. I'll have a (brandy). |
| What would you like to drink? | A glass of red wine, please. |
| Would you like a beer? / a whisky? / some juice? | Yes, please. |
| | No, thank you. I'm fine |

### Looking at the menu

This looks good.
I'm not familiar with these dishes. Can you recommend something?
Is there a vegetarian dish?
What's ('tête de veau')? [*indicating something on the menu*]

### Ordering

| *Waiter* | *Customer* |
|---|---|
| Would you like to order now? | I'd like (the casserole), please. |
| | I'll have the (chicken) with vegetables, please. |
| | I'll have (rice). |
| | I'll have (a salad). |
| | I think I'll try the (salmon). |
| | Can you tell me what's in the (vegetable) dish? |
| | What kind of (meat) is that? |

| | | |
|---|---|---|
| Would you like | some coffee? | Yes, please |
| | sauce with that? | No, thank you. |
| | wine? | Later, please. |

### During the meal

| | |
|---|---|
| How's your meal? | Fine. |
| | Excellent. |
| | It's delicious. |
| | Quite good. |
| Is the (chicken) all right? | Yes, it's fine. |
| | Well, it's a bit cold. |
| | Well, it's a bit undercooked. |
| Here, have some more wine. | No, thank you. |
| Would you like more salad? | Yes, please. |
| Would you like to try the fish? | |

### At the end

That was great!
I really enjoyed that.
Thank you. That was delicious.

### Offering to pay

It is usually clear from the context who is going to pay for a meal in a restaurant – normally the person who has invited you. You may, however, wish to pay for a drink for yourself and your host.

I'll get this. [*picking up the bill, or at the bar*]
This is on me.
Really, I insist.

## *Small talk*

In social situations you need to be able to make 'small talk' ie. general conversation about neutral subjects. This helps people to feel comfortable and develop their relationship. Below are some examples of topics, questions and responses to help your conversation skills.

### Hotel

| | |
|---|---|
| Is your hotel comfortable? | Yes, it's fine, thanks. |
| I hope your hotel is comfortable. | Yes, it's really good. There's a (wonderful view from my room). |

### Journey

Did you have a good trip?

How long did it take you to get here?
When did you get here?
Are you going straight home to (Madrid) after this?
Is this your first visit to (London)?

### Weather

What's the weather like in (Washington) at this time of year?
So, what do you think of the weather here?

### Places

Have you ever been to (Norway)?
Have you ever seen (the Statue of Liberty)?
Can you tell us something about (your town)?
Do you like living in (Singapore)?

### Opinions

What do you think of (the food)?
Do you think (the new recruitment policy) is a good idea?
Do you like (the changes we've made to the office)?

## *Thanking*

### General situations

Thank you very much.
Thank you. That's very kind of you.
Thank you for a very enjoyable evening.
I'd like to thank you for all your help.
I'd just like to say thank you for a great day.

### Response to thanks

That's okay.
You're very welcome.
Don't mention it.
It was a pleasure.
I'm glad you enjoyed it.

## *Apologizing*

You may find yourself in a situation where you need to apologize, eg. you arrive late at a meeting or you have forgotten or misunderstood something.

I'm sorry.
I'm very sorry.
I'm sorry I'm late.
I'm terribly sorry | for the delay
| that I missed the meeting.

### Responses

That's all right.
Don't worry about it.
Never mind.

# 7

# Marketing, advertising and sales

Many people use the words **marketing**, **sales** and **advertising** interchangeably. However, the word 'marketing' refers to an overall approach to doing business, while sales and advertising are specific activities that form part of the marketing process. Other such activities are market research and new product development.

**Marketing** involves analysing and understanding customer needs in order to enable the company to provide the most appropriate products and services.

**Advertising** is communicating the company's message and promoting its products, services and ideas to existing or potential customers.

**Sales** is the process of persuading people to buy the company's products.

## Word partnerships: market

The term **market** refers to the actual or potential demand for a product. A company's or product's target market is the group of people a company aims to sell its products to, for example university students, children, homeowners, people over 65.

Below are some words which commonly occur after **market**:

| | |
|---|---|
| market ... | research<br>share<br>segment<br>niche<br>leader |

**Market research** is the collection and study of data about a market, carried out in order to make decisions about products. **Market share** is the percentage of sales that a company or product has in a particular market.

A **market segment** is a distinct group of buyers, identified by characteristics such as income, age, lifestyle, preferences and geographical area. A **market niche** is a small, specific segment of the market, often dominated by small firms selling specialized or luxury goods.

A **market leader** is the company or product with the largest share in a particular market.

*We need to do more* ***market research*** *before we decide on the packaging for the perfume.*
*We aim to expand our total* ***market share*** *in the luxury pen market by March next year.*
*A seller needs to target the most suitable* ***market segment*** *for its products.*
*The company now commands a* ***market niche,*** *selling to naturalists and birdwatchers.*
*Microsoft is the* ***market leader*** *in software.*

## Key phrases: marketing

| | |
|---|---|
| marketing strategy | SWOT analysis |
| marketing plan | marketing audit |
| marketing environment | marketing mix |

**Marketing strategy** refers to a company's overall approach to achieving its marketing objectives. A **marketing plan** is a document giving a detailed explanation of how a company will achieve its marketing objectives for a particular product.

The **marketing environment** includes all the factors affecting a market; the macro-environment refers to factors affecting the whole economy and the micro-environment refers to factors affecting individual markets and areas. A **SWOT analysis** is a method of examining a company's **S**trengths and **W**eaknesses, and the **O**pportunities and **T**hreats it encounters in the market.

An evaluation of a company's marketing objectives, strategies, environment and activities is known as a **marketing audit**. The **marketing mix** describes the various factors a company must take into consideration when developing its marketing objectives (see the section **The marketing mix** below).

*Next week's meeting will concentrate on the **marketing strategy**.*
*The board did not accept the **marketing plan**. We need to clarify our objectives.*
*The marketing department is researching the **marketing environment**.*
*The **SWOT analysis** was particularly useful in clarifying our position in the domestic market.*
*The results of the **marketing audit** led the firm to make radical changes to their research methods.*
*We need to re-examine the **marketing mix**, particularly our pricing.*

## The marketing mix

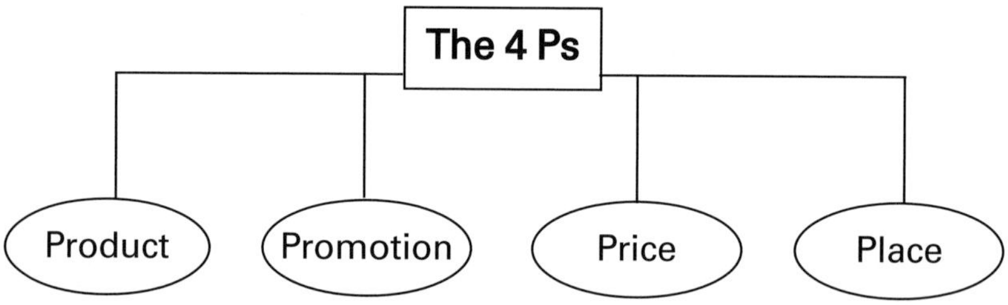


Below is a selection of many of the words and phrases that you will come across in relation to the marketing mix.

### *Product*

A **product** can be defined as 'anything that can be marketed', and includes physical objects, services, ideas, and even people. Below are some commonly-used words and terms relating to the product:

| | |
|---|---|
| position | brand |
| product portfolio | branding |
| product launch | brand switcher |
| premium product | brand loyalty |
| packaging | family brands |
| research and development | own-label brands |

**position (something)**
to decide where to place a product in relation to its competitors: *The department store positions itself as a high-quality, high-status retailer.*

**product portfolio**
the range of products or services offered by a company: *We need to take a look at our product portfolio, and improve our offer of low-priced units.*

**product launch**
putting a new product into the market: *The product launch was covered by the regional press.*

**premium product**
a product positioned at the top end of the market: *Imported beers are usually positioned as premium products.*

**packaging**
a product's wrapper or container: *The marketing department will specify the type of packaging that will appeal to prospective customers.*

**research and development (R&D)**
The process of designing new products and improving existing ones: *The R&D department is in Hamburg.*

**brand**
a name, term, symbol or sign that identifies a product: *Calvin Klein is one of the best-known brands of jeans.*

**branding**
a way of differentiating products by building a brand around them: *Decisions about branding affect our investment in promotion and packaging.*

**brand switcher**
buyers who change brands regularly: *Sales promotions are particularly effective in attracting brand switchers.*

**brand loyalty**
sticking to a known brand regardless of the competition: *In the war between the major soap-powder producers, brand loyalty has been a major factor.*

**family brands**
products of a company which all carry the same name, eg. Microsoft, Yamaha, Del Monte: *Ford is one of the world's best-known family brands.*

**own-label brands**
products sold under the name of a supplier or retailer: *Own-*

*label brands now account for a large proportion of the supermarket's turnover.*

## Price

**Price**, the second element in the marketing mix, refers to how much money a company charges for its products.

| | |
|---|---|
| pricing policy | discount pricing |
| markup | loss leader pricing |

### pricing policy
a company's approach to setting prices: *A company needs to consider its long- and short-term pricing policies.*

### markup
a percentage added to the cost of producing a product or providing a service: *A forty per cent markup was recommended by the wholesalers.*

### discount pricing
reducing the price of a product to attract buyers and/or clear stock: *A large volume of sales is needed to make discount pricing successful.*

### loss leader
a product which is sold at a loss to attract buyers who will then buy other goods: *Canned beans are this week's loss leader.*

## Place

**Place** refers to distribution, that is, how and where the product is made available to customers. The company must decide on (i) which are likely to be the most effective kinds of outlets, (ii) the most cost-effective means of distribution, and (iii) which production issues will affect distribution, for example, the type of container that is used for a product, or the size of the product or the packaging.

## Channel of distribution

This is the route a product takes on its way to the customers, each stage adding a markup on the price. A typical channel of distribution for a manufactured product is shown below:

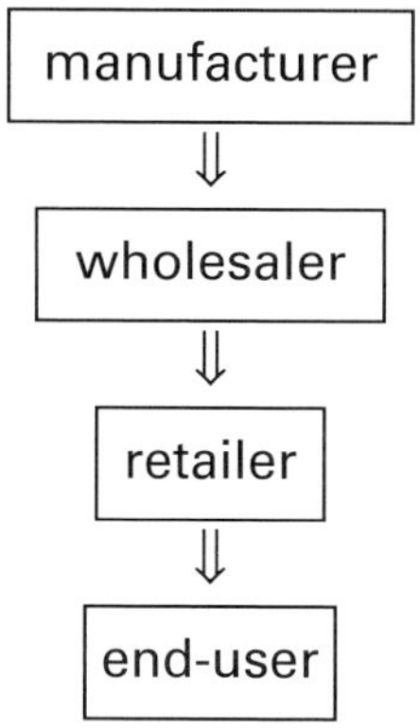


| | |
|---|---|
| **plant** | **factory outlet** |
| **warehouse** | **mail order** |
| **wholesaler** | **overseas agent** |
| **retailer** | **transportation** |
| **outlet** | |

### plant
a factory: *The new food-processing plant has provided two hundred jobs for the area.*

### warehouse
a large building where goods are kept: *Our main warehouses are close to the docks.*

### wholesaler
a company that buys in large quantities from manufacturers, to sell on to retailers: *I'm afraid we've run out of this model. We'll have to order some more from the wholesaler.*

### retailer
a company which sells goods directly to the customer in shops and stores: *Marks and Spencer is one of the UK's best-known retailers.*

### outlet
a place, such as a shop, where goods are sold to the public: *They plan to open a new outlet every month for the next three years.*

### factory outlet
a shop where a plant sells its products directly to the public: *Clothing manufacturers do a good trade through factory outlets.*

### mail-order
a method of selling, using catalogues and the postal service: *The number of mail-order firms is on the increase in the UK.*

**overseas agent**
a company that sells another company's products in foreign markets: *Could you send this report to all our overseas agents, please?*

**transportation**
methods of delivering goods to target markets: *Air-freight is the most cost-effective method of transportation for our South American orders.*

## *Promotion*

The term **promotion** refers to communicating with, and influencing, customers to buy your products. It involves creating a clear identity and image for a product and bringing the product's benefits to the customers' notice. The major promotional tools are:

| | |
|---|---|
| **sales force** | **public relations** |
| **advertising** | **sales promotions** |

**sales force**
the people in the sales department who sell a company's products: *Each member of the sales force is responsible for two or three products.*

**advertising**
paying to promote products, services, events and people through TV and radio commercials, the Internet, magazines and other media: *We decided to increase the advertising budget by twenty per cent.*

**public relations (PR)**
communicating a positive image of a company through articles, press releases, parties and other events: *She's been working in PR for ten years.* ❑ *We're organizing a big PR event to accompany the launch of our new product.*

**sales promotions**
ways of stimulating sales of a product eg. offering free samples: *The 'two-for-the-price-of-one' offer has been our most successful sales promotion so far this month.*

## Market research

Marketing managers need to collect specific information about markets, and may commission market research companies to carry out these studies. Here are some of the terms you are likely to come across when reading or talking about market research:

| | |
|---|---|
| **sample** | **primary data** |
| **questionnaire** | **secondary data** |
| **survey** | **findings** |
| **focus group** | |

A **sample** is a small part of the population, which is taken to represent the whole.

A **questionnaire** is a set of questions used in a **survey** to find out about people's opinions, behaviour and practices. Market research is often carried out through a **focus group**. A focus group is a number of people who take part in a carefully managed discussion, in order to provide data about attitudes and responses to products and services. Original data like this is called **primary data**, while information collected from periodicals, government publications, online databases and other sources is known as **secondary data**. The results of market research are known as **findings**. These are presented at the end of the research task.

*A **sample** of women between the ages of twenty and thirty was interviewed.*

*Because of errors in the **questionnaire**, the results of the **survey** were invalid.*

*A **focus group** of eight people discussed the image of the company's products.*

*The **primary data** suggests that there is a slowdown in this market.*

*Could you check the Internet for sources of **secondary data**?*

*As a result of the **findings**, the research and development department proceeded with their plans for a new model.*

### *The process*

Below are the steps market researchers take when carrying out market research.

1. identify the problem or the opportunity and the research objectives

2 decide on the research methods (eg. focus group, survey)
3. decide on the research instrument (questionnaire)
4. choose contact methods (mail, telephone, Internet, personal interview)
5. collect data
6. analyse data
7. present findings

## *Designing a questionnaire*

When designing a questionnaire (the most commonly-used market research instrument), the market researcher needs to choose questions very carefully, considering the form, the wording and the sequence. Closed questions are designed to limit the number or types of answers that can be given. Open questions allow the respondent to give opinions and reasons more freely. Here are some types of question that can be included in a questionnaire:

### Questions designed to obtain a single answer:

- Do you buy your own magazines?

  yes ☐ no ☐

- Who do you live with?

  nobody ☐
  friends ☐
  parents ☐
  relatives ☐
  other (please specify) ☐

### Scaled question

This type of question offers statements with which the respondent can show the amount of agreement or disagreement, or that rates the importance of something, eg. from poor to excellent.

- 'Teenage magazines are expensive.' Select the response that is closest to your opinion:

  strongly agree ☐
  agree ☐
  neither agree nor disagree ☐
  disagree ☐
  strongly disagree ☐

## Prioritizing question

A prioritizing question asks the respondents to rank certain points according to their personal preferences.

❍ Place the following in order of importance to you.

photos of music stars ☐
letters page ☐
cosmetics advice ☐
true stories ☐
problem page ☐
main feature ☐
advertisements ☐

## Open question

An open question asks the respondent to write freely on the subject, allowing for any opinions to be given that were not picked up earlier.

❍ What is your opinion of this magazine?

❍ Complete this sentence: 'What I like about this magazine is …'.

# Advertising

Advertising is one of the main methods of promotion, involving informing consumers about products, and attempting to persuade them to buy. Below are some words which are commonly used to talk about the world of advertising:

| | |
|---|---|
| **advertising agency** | **brief** |
| **account** | **medium** |
| **advertising campaign** | **medium, media (pl)** |
| **budget** | **advertisement** |

Large companies usually use **advertising agencies** to promote their products and the company's image to the target customers.

The **account** is the contract between the client company and the agency to develop an **advertising campaign**. The client allocates a **budget**, an amount of money, to the task. The agency and the client then discuss the **brief**, which is a statement of the client's objectives, as well as the message the company wishes to communicate to the consumers.

Once this has been agreed, the agency is ready to start work, deciding which **medium** to use, for example television, radio, newspapers. The agency then creates the **advertisements**.

*He works for one of the big **advertising agencies** in London.*
*She is responsible for the Smith **account**.*
*The **advertising campaign** was launched on the first of June.*
*With this **budget** we can't even consider TV commercials.*
*The client's **brief** stated that the advertising should target the 20–30 age group.*
*The choice of **media** open to us is limited by the budget.*
***Advertisements** in the national press for computer systems have been particularly effective.*

> ⓘ Advertisements are often referred to as 'ads' or 'adverts'.
> ❍ The concepts of 'advertising' and 'publicity' are sometimes confused, but they have different meanings. Advertising is paid for by the company, while 'publicity' simply means 'notice or attention from the media', which can be good or bad for a company's reputation.

## *Media used in advertising*

The medium that a company uses to advertise its product is influenced by factors such as budget, objectives and the target market. Below are the most common types of advertising media available to a company (see explanations below).

**Printed material**
brochures
leaflets
catalogues
flyers
inserts

**press**
newspapers
magazines

**broadcasting**
TV
cinema
radio

**electronic**
Internet (eg. websites and e-mail)

**display**
posters
hoardings/billboards
public transport
point of sale

**others**
trade fair
sponsorship
word-of-mouth
packaging

### Explanations

**brochure**: a small booklet

**leaflet**: a folded sheet of printed paper

**catalogue**: a book containing details of items for sale

**flyer**: a small piece of paper, often delivered to homes

**insert**: advertising material which is delivered inside a newspaper as a separate sheet

**hoarding (*BrE*), billboard (*AmE*)**: a large board for displaying posters alongside roads

**point of sale**: the place where a customer buys something eg. a shop or a showroom

**trade fair**: an exhibition where companies in a particular industry display their products to potential buyers

**sponsorship**: money given by a company for sports, for the arts, or for some other event, in order to gain publicity

**word-of-mouth**: free advertising through satisfied customers telling their friends about a product or service

# Sales

## Word partnerships: sales

The words below commonly occur after 'sales':

| | |
|---|---|
| sales ... | **representative**<br>**force**<br>**territory**<br>**forecast**<br>**targets**<br>**campaign**<br>**promotion**<br>**literature** |

A person who sells to customers is called a salesman, saleswoman, salesperson or **sales representative**, often shortened to **sales rep**. All the sales representatives of a company are called the **sales force**. The geographical area covered by a sales rep is known as his or her **sales territory**.

Within a company, the sales department is responsible for **sales forecasts**, ie. predicting the number of future sales in a certain period, and setting **sales targets** for a particular area or period.

As part of a **sales campaign**, a drive to boost sales, customers are frequently offered **sales promotions** such as price reductions and free gifts. Printed information for customers is called **sales literature**.

*Layton Thomas is looking for enthusiastic **sales representatives** to join its sales force.*
*Her **sales territory** includes both counties.*
*Joe will now present the **sales forecasts** for the next quarter.*
*Unfortunately, the **sales campaign** failed to make a significant impact on the sales figures for the period.*
*The planned series of **sales promotions** will enable us to meet the sales target for this year.*
***Sales literature** helps you to communicate information about the company's products and services.*

## The sales representative

The job of the sales representative is not simply to sell a product or service. The main responsibilities are outlined below.

- to find new customers
- to develop customer relations
- to support customer service
- to deliver point-of-sale material
- to leave samples
- to provide product updates
- to give new product information
- to liaise between company and customers

## Sales promotions

The purpose of sales promotions is to attract customers to buy a product or service by communicating its benefits and offering a special incentive. Here are some common types of sales promotion with specific examples:

| *Promotion* | *examples* |
|---|---|
| competitions | contests eg. to write a slogan |
| free gifts | pens, badges, bags, cosmetics, toys |
| samples | food, shampoo, perfumes |

| ***Promotion*** | ***examples*** |
| --- | --- |
| demonstrations | cosmetics, domestic appliances |
| trading stamps | supermarkets, petrol |
| price reductions | sales, special offers |
| coupons | household cleaning goods, holidays, hotels |
| discounts | two for the price of one, bulk-buying |

# 8

# Employment

Work plays a major part in most people's lives, and in recent years many people's working environment has changed radically. As the labour market becomes more flexible, many employers respond by increasing the number of fixed-term contracts and part-time workers.

The Human Resources department of a company is responsible for planning, recruitment of new people, staff training and development, staff appraisal, welfare, pensions administration and industrial relations. It works to ensure that the right people are available to meet the company's needs.

## Basic terms

| | |
|---|---|
| employment | out of work |
| work (noun) | on the dole |
| job | self-employed |
| position | work freelance |
| post | voluntary work |
| unemployed | |

### employment
having a paid job: *The fastest growing sector in the labour market is in the employment of women.*

### work
what you do to earn money: *Could you tell me about the kind of work you are looking for?*

### job
work done regularly, usually to earn money; an occupation: *He's got a highly-paid job in the oil business.*

**position**
a job: *How many applications have we received for the position of Production Manager?*

**post**
a job: *I believe we have a suitable post for him in our Chicago office.*

**unemployed (*adjective*)**
without a job: *How long have you been unemployed?*

**the unemployed (*noun*)**
people without jobs: *The Government provides incentives to the unemployed to start their own businesses.*

**out of work**
without a job: *Hundreds of people have been out of work since the closure of the Japanese electronics plant.*

**on the dole (*BrE, colloquial*)**
registered unemployed and receiving benefit from the state: *He's been on the dole since the plant closed last year.*

**self-employed**
having your own business: *The 1980s saw rapid growth in the numbers of self-employed in the UK.*

**work freelance (*verb*)**
to work, often for more than one employer, and be paid separately for each piece of work: *She works freelance as a financial journalist.*

**voluntary work**
unpaid work, usually for a charity: *Many people like to include voluntary work on their CV.*

> ⓘ The term 'Human Resources Management' is increasingly replacing the term 'Personnel Management'.
> - **work** is an uncountable noun; *After graduation, she hopes to find work overseas.*
> - **job** is a countable noun; *After graduation, she hopes to find a job overseas.*

## Word partnerships: job

'Job' is commonly used in combination with the words below:

| | |
|---|---|
| job ... | description<br>title<br>sharing<br>analysis<br>rotation<br>satisfaction<br>security<br>advertisement |

A **job title** describes the function of a job, for example 'Sales Manager'.

An outline of the major responsibilities of a job is called a **job description**. A **job analysis** is carried out to examine a particular job in detail.

When a position is vacant, an organization puts a kind of notice, a **job advertisement**, in a newspaper, company bulletin or on the Internet.

Some companies move their workers regularly between teams or departments. This is known as **job rotation**. When two people do a single job between them it is known as **job-sharing**. **Job security** is knowing or feeling that a job will last for a long time, and **job satisfaction** is a feeling of contentment and achievement which comes from a job.

*This badge shows your name, the company name and your **job title**.*

*His experience and qualifications match the **job description** very well.*

*We've requested a **job analysis** to help us make decisions about the future of this post.*

*There are several **job advertisements** for administrative staff in today's newspaper.*

***Job rotation** has enabled our staff to broaden their range of skills.*

*Our company believes in the value of **job-sharing**, both for employees and the business.*

*Personal financial planning has been made difficult by the lack of **job security** in the modern workplace.*

*Although the pay is quite low, there is a high level of* ***job satisfaction****.*

ⓘ Use capitals for specific job titles. Compare *'He's the Sales Manager at Winton Electronics'* and *'I think he's a sales manager'*.

## Human Resources: the people

'Human Resources' means people, plus the skills and experience they bring to an organization. Job titles such as 'Accounts Manager' or 'Personal Assistant' define what people do, while the following words describe people's roles in more general terms:

| | |
|---|---|
| employer | staff |
| boss | employee |
| manager | worker |
| supervisor | white-collar worker |
| personnel | blue-collar worker |
| workforce | colleague |

An **employer** is a person or company that provides jobs. **Boss** is an informal word meaning 'someone in authority', for example an employer or owner of a company, or simply someone in a superior position. The person who runs a specific part of an organization is called a **manager**. The job title will depend on the area of responsibility, for example 'Production Manager'. Someone who is in charge of making sure a job is well done eg. on the factory floor, or in retailing, is sometimes called a **supervisor**.

**Personnel**, **workforce** and **staff** are general terms used to talk about the people who work for an organization.

**Employees** and **workers** are the people who work in an organization. Professionals or people who work in offices are **white-collar workers**, while manual workers such as factory workers are called **blue-collar workers**.

Someone who works with you in your job is a **colleague** (sometimes called a co-worker).

*NTF is an equal opportunities* ***employer****.*
*I'll have a word with the* ***boss*** *about leaving early this afternoon.*
*Could you report to the Marketing* ***Manager****, please?*
*If you have any problems please talk to your* ***supervisor****.*

*We cannot afford to lose skilled* ***personnel****.*
*The* ***workforce*** *has been reduced by half in the last ten years.*
*In Siemens, the number of overseas* ***staff*** *has increased by forty thousand in the last eighteen months.*
*All the company's* ***employees*** *are encouraged to take part in training courses.*
***White-collar workers*** *are most likely to be affected by the merger.*
*Health and safety regulations state that all* ***blue-collar workers*** *must be issued with a uniform.*
*Many of her* ***colleagues*** *are less well qualified than she is.*

## Recruitment procedure

Recruitment is the process of employing new people. This process will vary from one organization to another. In a small company, for example, it may be done quite informally, while a large corporation will have established procedures. The chart below shows the steps of a typical staff recruitment process.

The job need is identified

⇓

The job description is written or updated

⇓

Advertisements are placed or agencies are contacted

⇓

Applicants respond to the advertisement

⇓

The applications are screened (see page 89)

⇓

A shortlist is drawn up

⇓

Interview invitations are sent

⇓

Candidates are interviewed

⇓

A suitable candidate is selected

⇓

A job offer is made

⇓

References are followed up

⇓

The job offer is accepted

⇓

The employment contract is signed

## Recruitment: the jobseeker's role

| | |
|---|---|
| jobseeker | résumé (*AmE*) |
| apply for a job | covering letter |
| application form | applicant |
| curriculum vitae (*BrE*) | |

A **jobseeker** is a person who is looking for a job. If you are a jobseeker and you are interested in a particular post, you may decide to **apply for the job**. The first step is to get an **application form** and a job description from the company. The next step is to complete the form and return it with your **curriculum vitae (CV**, *BrE*) or **résumé** (*AmE*), which is a summary of your work history, education, and skills. You should also send a **covering letter**, supporting your CV. By doing this you have become an **applicant**.

*Local government offices have set up a telephone advice line for* ***jobseekers****.*
*In the last three months I have* ***applied for*** *six jobs.*
*Could you send me an* ***application form*** *and a job description please?*
*Please send your application, including a* ***CV****, to the address below.*
*Please send a full CV with a* ***covering letter*** *stating your current salary.*
*A total of ten* ***applicants*** *have been invited for interviews.*

## Curriculum vitae (résumé)

A well-written CV (or résumé) is a vital part of any job application and makes an immediate impression on the people making the selection. A CV should be targeted at a particular position or company, and should aim to show how the candidate can be an asset to that organization.

Here are some suggestions to help you write a CV in English, but remember that in different countries there may be different practices. For example, you may decide that it is not important to include your marital status in a CV, but in some countries employers will expect to see it.

### *Contents of a CV*

- **personal details**: name, address, telephone, e-mail, date of birth, nationality (if required), marital status (if required).

- **professional experience**: focus on your responsibilities and achievements rather than just names of companies and dates. Start with your most recent position and work backwards.

- **education and qualifications**: don't go back too far unless it's important to your application; recent graduates should pick out achievements eg. positions of leadership, evidence of successful teamwork whilst at university.

- **skills**: emphasize your skills, for instance, computing, languages, driving.

- **interests**: include only what will be viewed positively by the employer.

- **referees**: give the names of two people you can trust to be positive about you, or simply state that references are available on request.

### *Style*

- Be concise. Keep it to one, or at most two, sides of a page.

- Use bulleted points rather than paragraphs.

## *CV/ résumé (experienced applicant)*

# Cameron Grant

Address:14/3 Greenknowe Ave., Potts Point, NSW 2055, Australia
Tel: 2883 455
e-mail: cgrant@alc.com
Nationality: Australian
Date of birth: 1 May 1965

**Work history**

1994 to date: International Business Manager, Haircare Ltd, Sydney
Producer of hair care products

*Responsibilities:*

- *marketing in Europe and the Far East*
- *packaging development and design input*
- *setting up and developing distribution network*
- *negotiating contracts with major retailers*

1987–1991: Overseas Marketing Manager, Fourstar International, Tokyo
Manufacturer of broadcasting equipment

- *formulated strategy, developed distribution network, dealt with agents and customers*
- *produced sales material*
- *represented company at trade fairs worldwide*

**Education**

1993 MBA, London Business School

1987 BA Economics and Japanese, Sydney University, Sydney, Australia

**Skills**

fluent Japanese
holder of pilot's licence, four hundred hours of flying

**Interests**

keen interest in flying
hiking
member of Greenpeace

## *CV/résumé (recent graduate)*

# Beverley Roberts

**Personal details**

| | |
|---|---|
| Address: | 122 Honor Oak Road, Forest Hill, London SE23 4NM |
| Tel: | 669 3439 |
| e-mail: | broberts@goserve.net |
| Nationality: | British |
| Date of birth: | 4 October 1976 |

**Education**

| | |
|---|---|
| 1999 | MSc Computing for Business and Industry, Napier University, Edinburgh |
| 1998 | BA Business Administration (2.2), University of South Wales |
| 1994 | Hull Grammar School. 'A' levels in Italian (A), Computer studies (A) and Economics (B) |

**Work experience**

| | |
|---|---|
| Summer 1998 | Website design, Hypercommunications Ltd, Cardiff<br>Member of corporate website design team |
| Summer 1996: | Adventure camp group leader, Nottingham<br>Responsible for sailing tuition |

**Skills**

- full driving licence
- fluent Italian
- experience of sailing training with under-sixteens
- first aid certificate

**Interests**

- member of university sailing team until graduation
- contributor of articles to yachting magazines
- keen painter with a strong interest in modern art

Names of referees available on request.

# Recruitment: the company's role

## *Advertising*

| | |
|---|---|
| vacancy | headhunter |
| employment agency | |

When a company identifies a need for new staff, they may advertise the **vacancy** in national newspapers, or may contact an **employment agency**, a private company that matches jobseekers (people looking for work) with jobs. If the vacancy is an executive or senior management position, then a consultant known as a **headhunter** may be engaged to approach suitable people in other companies.

*She was promoted when a **vacancy** came up in the Kuala Lumpur office.*
*I've contacted several **employment agencies**, without any results.*
*She rejected approaches from several **headhunters**, but decided to stay in her present position as Head of Sales.*

## *Screening the applicants*

| | |
|---|---|
| application | shortlist |
| screening process | candidate |

Once the organization has received the jobseekers' **applications**, the **screening process** begins: reading through the applications and rejecting those that are unsuitable. The result of this process is a **shortlist** of applicants who will move on to the next stage. A person who is invited for an interview becomes a **candidate**.

*We received hundreds of **applications** for only two positions.*
*After we receive the applications, the **screening process** can begin.*
*Eight applicants are on the **shortlist** and have been contacted.*
*All the **candidates** on the shortlist have an MBA.*

# Interviewing

| | |
|---|---|
| interview | accept a job offer |
| interviewee | turn down a job offer |
| interviewer | appoint someone |
| reference (*BrE*) | employment contract |
| testimonial (*AmE*) | |

An **interview** is a formal meeting between a candidate and people from the company. In this situation, the candidate is the **interviewee** and the representatives of the company are the **interviewers**. After an interview, the interviewers will follow up the **references** or testimonials of promising candidates. To do this they ask for a letter about the candidate from a previous employer (or a tutor, in the case of a recent graduate).

Once this process has been completed, the interviewers need to select the best candidate for the job and offer him or her the post. The candidate will then **accept**, or **turn down**, **the job offer**. When the person has been officially **appointed** (given the job), an **employment contract** is signed, agreeing the working conditions and salary.

*The **interview** will last for about forty minutes.*
*Could you supply me with a **reference** for Joseph Okuda, please?*
*Well, have you **accepted the job offer**?*
*Why did you **turn down the job offer** in that property firm?*
*In her early thirties, she was **appointed** head of Public Relations.*

## *The job interview*

Most interviews are conducted by a panel of interviewers, ie. more than one person.

### Checklist for interviewers

- Decide in advance how the candidates will be assessed.
- Plan how the interview will be conducted.
- Make a list of questions and decide who will ask them.
- Read the applications carefully beforehand.

- Help the candidates to relax by making small-talk.
- Explain what will happen in the interview.
- Ask open-ended questions.
- Leave time for the candidate to ask questions at the end.
- Explain when and how the candidate will be told the result of the interview.

### Checklist for interviewees

- Research the organization in advance.
- Read the job description carefully.
- Think about the questions you may be asked, and plan your responses.
- Be prepared to talk about your career, both past and future.
- Be ready to explain why you think you are suitable for the job.
- Practise with someone beforehand if you are nervous.
- Ask questions.

## *Job interview questions*

Some questions asked by interviewers at interviews are job-specific, relating to a particular post or field of work. Others are of a more general nature and encourage the candidate to talk about work experience, future goals and reasons for applying for the post. Open-ended questions give the interviewees the opportunity to express themselves, and give the interviewers the chance to assess the candidates' responses.

Below are some questions that are frequently asked in job interviews:

- Why do you want to join this company?
- What do you think you can | bring to this job?<br>| contribute to this job?
- What changes would you implement if you got this job?
- How would you feel about | relocating to (Malaysia)?<br>| working in a very small team?<br>| developing communications training courses?

- Could you tell us something about your responsibilities in your last job? / long term goals? / experience of dealing with difficult clients?
- What has brought you to this point in your career?
- What would you say are your strengths? / weaknesses?
- How would you deal with (a dissatisfied customer)? / handle (the following situation) …?
- What do you see yourself doing in five years?
- How do you see yourself developing personally?

## Money

Towards the end of an interview it may be appropriate to discuss money and fringe benefits, though the finer details will usually be discussed when the job offer is made.

| | |
|---|---|
| **income** | **remuneration** |
| **salary** | **commission** |
| **wages** | **fee** |

The money a person receives, including salary, dividends, interest, and rent on properties is called **income**. In the workplace, a white-collar worker receives an annual **salary** which is paid monthly, while a blue-collar worker receives a weekly payment called **wages**. **Remuneration** is a general term meaning 'payment for work'. In some jobs (in sales for example), the employee receives a **commission**, which is a percentage of the amount he or she has sold. A **fee** is money paid for the professional services of people such as lawyers, consultants and architects.

*His total **income** for this year including dividends and fringe benefits is expected to reach $250,000.*
*What **salary** were you offered?*
*Workers faced a drop in **wages** as recession hit Japan.*
*We offer an excellent **remuneration** and benefits package to the right candidate.*
*This post offers a basic salary plus generous **commission**.*
*Lawyers' **fees** will have to be paid by the end of this month.*

## Fringe benefits

perks
benefits package
private medical insurance
company pension scheme
share options

Fringe benefits or **perks** are extras received by an employee in addition to wages or salary. In managerial positions these are usually generous, and are negotiated when a job offer is being made. A **benefits package** may include some of the following: a company pension scheme, **private medical insurance**, company car, share options. A **company pension scheme** is a private pension plan which the employer (and often the employee) contributes to. **Share options** give the employee the chance to buy shares in the company at a reduced rate.

*One of the more enjoyable **perks** of the job is being able to use the gym in the basement.*
*The salary and **benefits package** are negotiable.*
*As well as a company car, we can offer you free **private medical insurance**.*
*You can join the **company pension scheme** immediately.*
*Company **share options** are seen as one of the most valuable fringe benefits.*

## Job responsibilities and company structure

Here is a simple diagram showing part of a company's hierarchy which is being explained to a new employee in the marketing department.

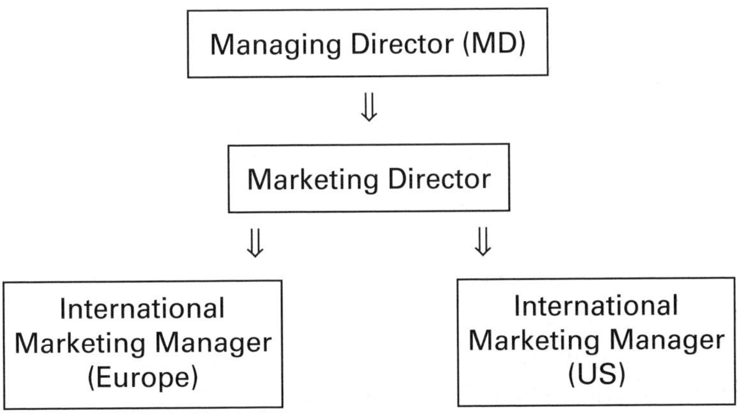

- The company is **headed by** the Managing Director, Victor Galloway.
- Paula Wells, the Marketing Director **is responsible for** the marketing department.
- Both marketing managers **report** directly **to** Paula.
- The International Marketing Manager for Europe, Judith Roca, is **in charge of** the promotional campaign in Poland.
- She is **assisted by** a marketing team of six people.
- Your team **is accountable to** the International Marketing Manager for the US, Alan Kotowski.

To **head** a company is to lead it. If you are under the authority of another person, you are **accountable to** them, or you **report to** them. To **assist** someone means to help or support them.

You are **in charge of** something, or **responsible for** it, if it is under your control.

## Changes in the workplace

Change in organizations occurs for social, political and economic reasons such as recession, privatization, mergers and takeovers. Companies respond to change in many ways, including the following:

| | |
|---|---|
| **restructuring** | **delayering** |
| **downsizing** | |

**restructuring**
changing the fundamental structure or shape of an organization or group: *The car industry in Europe has undergone massive restructuring in recent years.*

**downsizing**
reducing the number of employees: *We see downsizing as our only option if the company is to remain competitive.*

**delayering**
reducing the number of levels of management: *As a result of delayering, the corporation now has a much flatter hierarchy.*

## Leaving a job

There are various ways to leave a job, some voluntary and some involuntary. The words and phrases below are commonly used to talk about leaving, or being forced to leave, a position:

| | |
|---|---|
| resign | retire |
| quit (a job, a post) | take early retirement |

You **resign**, or you **quit** your job, when you choose to leave it. At the age of sixty or sixty-five many employees **retire**, though the retirement age varies from one country to another. Some employees leave at an earlier age; this is known as **taking early retirement**.

*Mr Russell, Director of the organic food retailer, **has resigned**.*
*Stephen Nicoli, chief executive of Greener Holidays is expected to **quit** his post as the company's share price continues to fall.*
*The Chairman has announced that he **will retire** in April on his sixty-fifth birthday.*
*Forty-seven workers in the factory have agreed to **take early retirement**.*

| | |
|---|---|
| redundancy | lay someone off |
| lay-off | redundancy payment |
| make someone redundant | |

Company reorganization, relocation or closure often result in job losses. These job losses are known as **redundancies** or **lay-offs**. An employee who is **made redundant** or **laid off** may receive a **redundancy payment**. This is an amount of money paid out to compensate the employee for the job loss, based on the number of years worked in the organization and the salary earned.

*Two thousand workers face **redundancy** in the semiconductor industry.*
*Four hundred workers will be **made redundant** over the next twelve months as the US parent company closes its UK operations.*
*She set up her own consultancy firm using her **redundancy payment**.*
*More **lay-offs** are predicted in the rail industry.*

*There are plans to **lay off** twenty per cent of the workforce.*

| | |
|---|---|
| **dismiss** | **sack** |
| **fire** | |

To terminate a contract of employment is to **dismiss**, **fire** or **sack** an employee.

*The union is calling for strike action after five drivers were **dismissed**.*
*Two people **were fired** after being caught stealing company products.*
*He **was sacked** for persistent lateness.*

## Industrial relations

'Industrial relations' refers to the relationship between management and workers. The human resources department deals with all aspects of this relationship, for example dismissals, conflicts, negotiations over pay and conditions. Key words in industrial relations include the following:

| | |
|---|---|
| **trade union** | **employers' association** |
| **labor union** | **strike** |
| **collective bargaining** | **industrial action** |
| **union representative** | **industrial dispute** |

### trade union (*BrE*)
### labor union (*AmE*)

an association of workers in one or more industries, formed to improve pay and working conditions through collective bargaining: *Trade unions in the UK, where membership has declined hugely in the last ten years, are working to recruit new members.*

### collective bargaining

negotiation between trade union and employer regarding pay and conditions: *In the 1980s more than fifty per cent of British workers' pay was decided through collective bargaining.*

### union representative

a person who is elected by union members to speak and act on their behalf: *Union representatives are meeting tomorrow to discuss the pay proposals.*

**employers' association**
an organization of employers formed to take part in the collective bargaining process: *The employers' association for manufacturers of building materials is called The Cement Makers' Federation.*

**strike**
to refuse to work, in protest against something: *Rail workers have voted to strike from the tenth of this month.*

**industrial action**
organized action such as a strike, taken by employees to protest against pay or conditions: *Workers at the MJI Chemical plant have called for industrial action to protest against recent dismissals.*

**industrial dispute**
a disagreement between employers and employees, generally about pay and working conditions: *Negotiations finally brought an end to the long-running industrial dispute at the factory.*

# 9

# Business correspondence

This chapter looks at the letters, faxes and e-mails that companies send and receive. A letter, fax or e-mail may be preferable to a telephone call when the sender wants to provide a written record of a message, and, in the case of letters and fax, present the image of the company with its letterhead and logo.

## Style

Broadly speaking, you can use the same kind of language in business letters, faxes and e-mails, although faxes and e-mails are often less formal than letters.

In all types of business correspondence you should be clear, concise and polite. When you use a formal tone, avoid short forms and contractions, such as *I've*, *doesn't*, *aren't*, *shouldn't*, as well as colloquial expressions, which are generally considered to be informal.

Punctuation should be kept to a minimum – no full stops in abbreviations and no commas in addresses, eg.

Mr Paul Wexford
4 Elm Ave
London
SW8 5NJ
UK

## Letters

### *Organization*

- Even a short letter usually contains at least three paragraphs. In the first paragraph you should explain the purpose of the letter, the second (and third and fourth if necessary) should give details, and the final paragraph should comprise a polite ending.

- Each paragraph should contain one main idea, and should consist of no more than three or four sentences.

## Layout

Nowadays, 'blocked style' is commonly used in business letters. 'Blocked style' is the practice of starting all new paragraphs at the left edge of the page. Opposite is an example of a letter written in blocked style.

## Addresses

- If you are not using pre-printed stationery, put the sender's address in the top right-hand corner of the page.
- Note that the sender's name only appears at the end of the letter, and not with the address.
- The name, address and position of the person you are writing to goes on the left-hand side.

## Reference numbers

- Use of reference numbers makes it easier to keep track of correspondence for both the sender and the recipient.

## Date

- The position of the date is not fixed. Look at the letters in this chapter to see where it can be placed.
- There are various ways to write the date but to avoid confusion always write the month as a word, not a number, eg: *4 October 1999*

## Subject heading

- The subject heading tells the reader what the letter is about; the simplest style is to use **bold** type, and to keep it short and simple, eg: **After-sales service**.

## Greetings

The greeting you choose depends on who you are writing to.

- You do not have a specific name: *Dear Sir/Madam*<br>*Dear Sir or Madam*
- Writing to a woman: *Dear Ms Wickham*
- Writing to a man: *Dear Mr Al-Farsi*
- Informal business contact: *Dear Maria*
- It is now common to use **Ms** to address women in business, regardless of whether they are married or not. You can use

# Forbes Plastics Ltd

7 Murrayburn Road, Glasgow G14 2RR, United Kingdom
*Tel:0141 427 9875* *Fax: 0141 427 9674*
e-mail: cic@forbes.co.uk

21 January 2000

James O'Brate
Purchasing Manager
Comsa SA
Bertran 67
Barcelona 08022
Spain

Our ref C4543
Your ref FH/55

Dear Mr O'Brate

**Catalogue and price list**

Thank you for your enquiry about our range of office storage products.

Please find enclosed our current catalogue and price list, which I am sure you will find of interest.

Our sales representative will be visiting customers in Spain next month and will be happy to meet you with samples of our products. I will contact you with more details in the near future.

If you require any further information, please do not hesitate to contact me.

Yours sincerely

*J. Nardini*

Joe Nardini
Sales Manager

**Mrs** and **Miss** to reply to correspondence where the writer signs herself **Miss** or **Mrs**. eg. You receive a letter from *Mrs Paula White* so you start your reply *'Dear Mrs White'.*

- Use **Mr**, **Ms**, **Mrs** and **Miss** with the surname only, not the first name, eg. You are writing to *Clive Harper* so you start *Dear Mr Harper.*
- In American English greetings, full stops are often used after **Mr, Ms, Miss** and **Mrs** and a colon (:) is placed after the name, eg. *Dear Mr. Williams.*

## *Closing a letter*

How you close your letter depends the greeting you have used. There are some differences between British and American English in this area, and these are shown below:

| | *Opening* | *Closing* |
|---|---|---|
| **British English** | | |
| | Dear Sir/Madam | Yours faithfully |
| | Dear Mr Gates | Yours sincerely |
| | Dear Ms Hughes | |
| **American English** | | |
| | Dear Sir/Madam | Sincerely yours<br>Truly yours<br>Respectfully yours |
| | Dear Mr. Gates<br>Dear Ms. Hughes | Yours sincerely<br>Sincerely yours<br>Yours truly<br>Truly yours |
| **British and American English** | | |
| | Dear Maya (informal) | Best wishes<br>Best regards<br>Kind regards |

## *Signature*

- The writer's name and position in the organization should be printed below the signature.

  eg. *Samuel Poynton*
  Samuel Poynton
  Financial Analyst

- **pp** is used to show that the letter has been signed by one person in place of another.

eg. *pp* *Julie Minato*
Samuel Poynton
Financial Analyst

The letters below are examples of the types of formal letters that you will send and receive in your business dealings. You can use these, along with the section on Essential Language of Business Correspondence, to help you write letters which are appropriate to your own situation.

## *letter requesting information*

**Novatel plc**

56 Hill Place, London SE4 8WT
Tel: 0171 485 7896 Fax: 0171 475 8383
e-mail admin@novatel.co.uk

Ms Emiko Nakamura — 12 May 2000
Training Manager
Novatel Japan
1-22-7 Shimada Mansions
Setagaya-ku
Tokyo 155
Japan

Dear Ms Nakamura

**Novatel 'Year 2001' conference**

As discussed, I am enclosing the schedule for the 'Year 2001' conference which will be held here in London from 22–26 July this year.

Could you please send me the names of the participants from your offices who will be attending, so that we can confirm hotel and local transport arrangements?

I look forward to hearing from you soon.

Yours sincerely

*Ailsa Macauley*

Ailsa Macauley
Organizer

## *letter of complaint*

EXCEL HOMES

10 Collins Gardens
Glasgow G52 5BL
Tel: 0141 443 0177
Fax: 0141 443 2230

Mr Jim Stephenson
T-Tiles Warehouse
4 Baxters Lane
Pontypridd
Mid Glamorgan
CF45 7SL

28 January 2000

Our ref: GR548
Your ref: TF-771

Dear Mr Stephenson

**Order 4543 – failure to deliver.**

I am writing to you in connection with the above order for terracotta tiles, which we placed on 1 December 1999.

Unfortunately, we have not yet received the delivery as promised. As it is now three weeks overdue we would be grateful if you could forward the goods as soon as possible.

I look forward to hearing from you.

Yours sincerely

*pp Angie Bell*

Valerie Lowe
Manager

## *letter of apology*

# T-Tiles Warehouse

4 Baxters Lane
Pontypridd
Mid Glamorgan
CF45 7SL

Our ref: TF-771 1 Feb 2000
Your ref: GR548

Ms Valerie Lowe
10 Collins Gardens
Glasgow G52 5BL

Dear Ms Lowe

**Order Number 4543 – delayed delivery**

Thank you for your letter of 28 January regarding the late delivery of your order.

I would like to apologize for the delay, and for the inconvenience this has caused. The problem has now been rectified and I am pleased to tell you that your order will be delivered to you on Monday 5 February.

Once again please accept my apologies.

Yours sincerely

*Jim Stephenson*

Jim Stephenson
Manager

## *Sales promotion letter*

**Maddra Tours Inc**

222 Fairfield Road
San Carlos
CA 94039
USA

Tel: 916-797-8423 Fax: 916-676-7863

---

Castle Holidays Ltd
43 Rosemount Crescent
Plymouth
PL8 5BT
UK

May 16, 2000

Dear Sir or Madam:

**Travel opportunities in the USA**

We are an established travel company operating in the United States and Mexico. Currently we are offering special prices on all groups of more than twenty people coming from the UK.

This is an excellent opportunity for UK tour operators to develop connections with a successful firm based in California, and with links all over the US and Mexico.

Please find enclosed a copy of our brochure with our compliments. If you wish to pursue our special offer, or require any further information, please contact us.

We look forward to hearing from you, and to our possible future partnership.

Yours truly,

*Petra Green*

Petra Green
Sales Director

# Fax

A fax cover-sheet is the page you send with details of the sender and the recipient and what the fax is about. Apart from the layout, a fax is like a letter, and the style you use depends on the purpose of the fax. For example, faxes which are sent within companies, or faxes between people who have built up a close business relationship are likely to be quite informal. However, if you are contacting someone for the first time, you can use the same style as a formal letter.

Most businesses use pre-printed fax cover-sheets. Here is an example of an informal fax from one business associate to another.

**BK Computers**

12D Elgin Street Industrial Estate
Maidstone, Kent MD34 6BN
Tel: 01622 727 9020
Fax: 01622 232 4431

**FAX**

| | |
|---|---|
| To: Adrian Alexander | Fax: 0114 226 7887 |
| From: Alan Simpson | Date: 24 July 2000 |
| Re: Office supplies | Pages: 3 |
| cc: | |

---

Hi Larry

It was good to see you at the trade fair in Frankfurt last week. We made some interesting contacts which I am following up at the moment.

As promised, I am sending you details of our new range of office supplies. Just let me know if you need any more information.

I'm sure I'll see you in September in Toronto.

Kind regards

Alan

## E-mail

While it is often true that e-mails are shorter and more informal than letters, the degree of formality depends on the relationship between the sender and recipient, and the reason for e-mailing. A more formal style is common in business, as e-mails may be kept as a record of communication. Generally speaking, formal e-mails are similar to letters, and informal ones are similar to speech.

### *Greetings and endings*

In a formal e-mail it is often a good idea to use the same greetings and endings as in a letter eg. *Dear Mr Russell* and *Yours sincerely*. If, however, the person replies in a more informal style, you may follow that style in your next message. Informal e-mails use the following greetings:

*Dear Diana*
*Hi Diana*
*Hi*
*(no greeting)*

and the following endings:

*Regards*
*Best wishes*
*Take care*
*All the best*
*(your name only, eg. 'Lesley')*

### *General tips*

- If you are unsure about which style to use in an e-mail, it is best to use a more formal style.
- Only use abbreviations and acronyms that you are sure will be known to the person you are e-mailing.
- In more informal e-mails you can respond to questions and queries by inserting your answers into the original message, which is then sent back to the original writer.

Opposite is an example of an e-mail from an IT manager to a website developer:

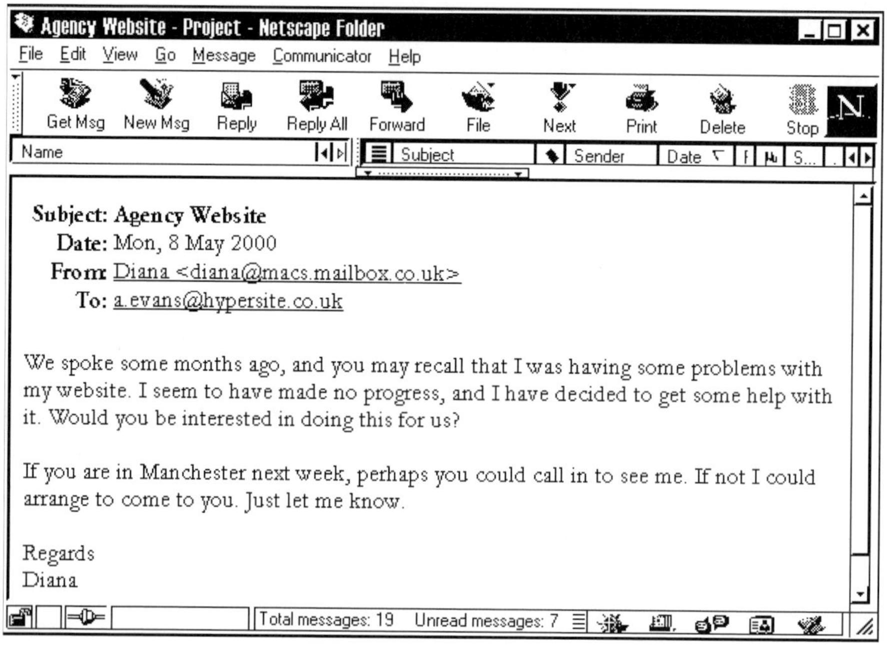


**Subject:** Agency Website
**Date:** Mon, 8 May 2000
**From:** Diana <diana@macs.mailbox.co.uk>
**To:** a.evans@hypersite.co.uk

We spoke some months ago, and you may recall that I was having some problems with my website. I seem to have made no progress, and I have decided to get some help with it. Would you be interested in doing this for us?

If you are in Manchester next week, perhaps you could call in to see me. If not I could arrange to come to you. Just let me know.

Regards
Diana

## Essential language of business correspondence

You can use the selection of phrases below to help you to write effective business letters, faxes and e-mails. The first five sections show various ways which in which a letter might begin.

### Referring

I refer to ... your application for the post of secretary (in the HR Department).

Further to ... our telephone conversation yesterday, (I am sending you the flight details).
... your letter of 22 June 1999, I am writing to (let you know that we are interested in your idea).

Thank you for your fax, which we received this morning.
As discussed, I am sending you the (1998 report).
As requested, here is the report (on the construction of the depot).

### Explaining the purpose

I am writing in connection with (the advertisement in the Guardian).

We are writing | in response to the (complaint we received from Mr Gary Mercer).
to enquire about (the handling of waste from Plant B).

| | |
|---|---|
| We are writing | in response to the (complaint we received from Mr Gary Mercer). |
| | to enquire about (the handling of waste from Plant B). |

I am pleased to inform you that (we can offer you the post of Personal Assistant).

### Describing your organization

We are a large TV cable manufacturer based in Frankfurt.
We are an established producer of knitwear products.
We are a financial services consultancy based in Los Angeles.

### Asking for something

| | |
|---|---|
| I would be grateful if you could | send me some information (about your water filters). |
| | contact us about this matter (immediately). |
| | forward your payment (as soon as possible). |
| Could you please send me a | price list? |
| | brochure? |

Could you please send me some information about (the conference)?

### Giving information and details

| | |
|---|---|
| Please find enclosed | payment for order number 9810/3C. |
| | a summary of my report. |

I am enclosing a copy of our invoice sent on 12 April.
I would like to inform you that (the arrangements have been finalized).
We are pleased to tell you about (our new range of products).
I am sorry to tell you that (we are unable to offer you a replacement).

### Saying what you can and cannot do

I will be able to (visit your office on Friday 23 June).
We can (arrange for a speedy delivery).
Unfortunately, I cannot (agree to the terms you suggest).
I am afraid we are unable to (offer you a full refund).

### Giving reasons

| | | |
|---|---|---|
| This is | due to | a shortage of (supplies). |
| | because of | a delay (in our production process). |
| | as a result of | |
| | owing to | |

### Making complaints

A complaint should always be made politely. First, the background should be explained, then the present situation, and finally, the person complaining should state what they want to see happen next, eg:

**background**: In our telephone conversation of 5 February, you promised delivery of order 3009 by the end of March.

**present situation**: Unfortunately I am still waiting for the goods.

**what you want to happen next**: I would be grateful if you could forward the goods immediately.

### Apologizing

I was sorry to hear about (the problems you have had with Model 898R).

We apologize for (the delay).

I regret any inconvenience this has caused you.

### Thanking

Thank you very much for (your help).

I would like to thank you for (the very enjoyable visit to York).

### Ending

If you require any further information, do not hesitate to contact me.

I look forward to hearing from you.

| | |
|---|---|
| We look forward to | doing business with you. |
| | receiving your order soon. |

# 10

# Report writing

A report is a document which contains information, facts and statistics. It may be a short one-page document or a more substantial piece of work which has taken many months to produce.

### *A good report*:

- is well researched and logically presented
- provides enough information to enable decisions to be made
- uses a style appropriate for the purpose (formal or informal)
- is accurate, clear and concise
- supports all claims and conclusions with evidence

### *Planning*

When planning a report there are two main points to consider:

- the purpose: why are you writing this report? Is the purpose clear?
- the readers: who will read it? What is their current knowledge of the subject? What do they need to know? What do they expect to be able to do with this report?

## A formal report

A formal report usually contains information based on research which is gathered by the report-writer. It is set out under headings and subheadings, which should be clearly numbered.

### *The process*:

request for a report ⇒ data collection ⇒ data selection ⇒

organization of data, visuals etc. ⇒ first draft ⇒

correct, omit, add, reorganize ⇒ summary ⇒ final draft

## Structure

Below is a typical pattern used for formal reports. However, note that organizations often have a 'house-style' (a style which is used by everybody in the organization) for reports and other documents.

Not all of the sections below are necessary for a short formal report, and some may be combined to form fewer sections. Also, the order in which they are presented may vary.

### *Title page*

This should include the subject of the report, the name of the report writer, the date, and if necessary a reference number or address.

### *Table of contents*

This is a list of all the headings and subheadings that are included in the report. They should be clearly numbered, as they appear in the report itself.

### *Summary*

In a long formal report it is usual to include a summary. The purpose of the summary is to focus the attention of the reader on the main conclusions of the report. The reader can get an overall view of the report by reading the summary along with the conclusions and recommendations. It can also help others decide whether or not they want to read the full report.

### *Terms of Reference*

The terms of reference describe the exact subject of the report, its scope and limitations, why it is being written and who asked for it. The procedure and the terms of reference together set the scene for the main part of the report.

Example:

*The purpose of this report is to analyse the advantages and disadvantages of relocating the head office of HJ Systems to Auckland, New Zealand, and to present its recommendations by 1 Sept 2000.*

## *Procedure*

This section explains the methods of investigation used to find the information, and the sources of this information. These may include:

- interviews
- meetings
- published sources
- observation
- visits
- questionnaires
- scientific measurement

Example:

*This report was compiled on the basis of:*

1. *information received from the NZ Dept of Trade and Industry regarding incentives for new businesses*
2. *discussions with the relevant unions in the UK*
3. *interviews with ten employees in HJ Systems UK*
4. *…*

## *Findings (main part)*

All the information that has been gathered is presented in this section. It is the longest part of the report, and is set out under headings and subheadings. This section should not contain the opinions of the writer, only facts and data. The findings should be presented in a logical order.

## *Conclusions*

In this section the writer states the significant results of the findings. There should be no new material here; the conclusions must flow logically from the facts and points raised in the findings.

Example:

*As a result of an analysis of the advantages and disadvantages of relocation to NZ, the following conclusions can be drawn:*

1. *Relocation would lead to approximately 90 job losses among the present staff.*
2. *Retraining costs in the new offices will reach approx NZ$50,000 in the first year.*
3. *Local government incentives to businesses in Auckland are generous but …*
4. *…*

### *Recommendations*

The writer recommends that specific actions should or should not be implemented, or indeed that nothing be done. Recommendations are based directly on the results of the investigation and must be supported by evidence. Nothing new should be included at this stage.

Example:

*Recommendations*

1. *Further discussions should be held with the NZ Dept of Trade and Industry in order to gain improved incentives.*
2. *Offers of voluntary redundancy should be offered to a maximum of 25 employees at the UK site.*
3. *UK premises should be offered for sale immediately.*
4. *...*
5. *...*

### *Appendices*

Information such as graphs, visuals, plans and so on, which have been included for reference, is attached to the report and should be clearly labelled Appendix A, B, C, etc.

### *Bibliography/References*

This section is a list of books, reports and other publications which have been referred to.

> ⓘ In a shorter report the *Terms of Reference* and *Procedure* are often combined to form the *Introduction*.
>
> - *Conclusions* and *Recommendations* may be joined to form one section called *Concluding Remarks* or *Conclusions and Recommendations*.

## Useful language for report writing

In a formal report the tone should be appropriate, as in other forms of written communication. Avoid short forms and contractions (using 'they will', not 'they'll', for example). Colloquial expressions and idioms are not suitable for formal writing in English.

The language points in this section will help you to write the details of your report.

## *Describing purpose*

| | |
|---|---|
| The purpose of this report is to | **examine** (the proposal)<br>**analyse**<br>**present**<br>**consider**<br>**review** |

This report aims to *analyse* (the advantages and disadvantages of the proposed expansion plans).

## *Use of the passive*

In a formal report you may want to avoid overuse of 'I'. You can, instead, put your verbs into the passive, making the report less personal.

Example:

Instead of *'I consulted Alastair Hill at the Dept of Trade and Industry'*, you can write *'Alastair Hill at the Dept of Trade and Industry* ***was consulted****'.*

Here are some more examples of this use:

*The department* ***is divided*** *into two sections.*
*Labour costs* ***were not taken*** *into account.*
*After discussion, the project* ***was given to*** *Glover Consultants Inc.*
*Two outer buildings* ***will be converted*** *into workshops.*
*It* ***was agreed*** *that flexible working hours* ***would be introduced*** *immediately.*
*The following observations* ***were made:*** *(firstly, the house owners were not insured for theft).*
*Offers of voluntary redundancy* ***have been made*** *to 120 employees.*
*It* ***is recommended*** *that further research* ***be undertaken****.*

## *Reporting what others have said*

In a report you may want to give an account of what others have said, for example, in a meeting. Below are some reporting verbs to choose from.

### Statements

| | |
|---|---|
| He<br>She | **said** that all building work was completed.<br>**stated** that extra staff had been taken on for the season. |

| | |
|---|---|
| The chairperson | **explained** that the figures would not be available until May. |
| The agent | **informed** the dealers that supplies would be delayed. |

### Requests

| | | |
|---|---|---|
| Mr King | **wanted to know**<br>**requested**<br>**asked for** | the details. |
| | **asked** the treasurer **for** the details. | |

### Replying

| | | |
|---|---|---|
| Twenty per cent of the participants | **replied to**<br>**answered** | the letter. |

### Agreeing and disagreeing

| | |
|---|---|
| Both parties | **agreed with** the decision.<br>**agreed that** the negotiation should be resumed.<br>**refused** the offer.<br>**accepted** that they had equal responsibility. |

### Opinions

| | |
|---|---|
| Margarita Lewis | **thought** that the profit could be increased<br>**felt**<br>**was of the opinion** |

## *Cause and effect*

You can link two pieces of information to show cause and effect.

| | | |
|---|---|---|
| Poor sales | **result in**<br>**cause**<br>**lead to**<br>**bring about** | poor profits |

The closure of two Korean manufacturing plants in the late nineties **led to** high regional unemployment.

January's fall in interest rates **resulted in** an upturn in the property market.

## *Giving reasons*

| | |
|---|---|
| The course was cancelled | **due to**<br>**because of**<br>**owing to**<br>**on account of**<br>**as a consequence of** |

... insufficient interest.

## *Showing contrast*

| | |
|---|---|
| although | whereas |
| even though | while |
| however | but |

***Although/Even though*** *the plant has enough space for production, storage has become a problem.*
*The plant has enough space for production.* ***However*** *storage has become a problem.*
*Our Mexican branch has reached its targets,* ***whereas*** *Spain is still 6% below.*
***While*** *we agree with you on the first two points, there is still a problem with the last one.*
*The local supplier is cheap,* ***but*** *there are problems with delivery.*

## *Classification*

When describing organizations, products, or stages of a project, it helps to be able to classify the different elements into categories. Here are some useful phrases:

| | |
|---|---|
| is made up of | is divided into |
| includes | comprises |
| consists of | contains |
| falls into | |

*Our range of services* ***is made up of*** *three types.*
*The project* ***consists of*** *five stages.*
*Our products* ***fall into*** *two categories.*
*The report* ***comprises*** *the background and the current problems.*
*The contract* ***contains*** *a clause about non-delivery of goods.*

## A short formal report

**To:** Julie Oliver, Managing Director
**From:** Alexander White, Training Manager
**Date:** 16 September 2000
**Subject:** Provision of in-house training courses.

**1. Introduction**

The purpose of this report is to examine the feasibility of holding all training courses in-house. External training providers were consulted, estimates of training costs were received, and comparative costs examined. Questionnaires were completed by 80 employees from four departments and 10 of the respondents were interviewed by members of the training department.

**2. Advantages**

**2.1** Following consultation with four of the company's regularly-used external training providers, it was calculated that in-house training would reduce the present cost by 26% in the first year (see Appendix A).

**2.2** It was felt by 65% of the staff that training courses could be better designed to suit the specific needs of the organization, and therefore bring benefit to the company as a whole.

**2.3** 45% of those who responded to the questionnaire felt that they were more likely to participate in training courses if they were held on-site.

**3. Disadvantages**

**3.1** Some respondents, particularly in the sales department, expressed concern that valuable business contacts arising from external training courses would be lost if all training was held in-house.

**3.2** Some training needs are very specific, and may only be required by one or two staff members. It was felt that these could not always be met by in-house training courses, as the necessary expertise could not always be brought in from outside.

**3.3** Participation in external training courses is seen by 30% of respondents as a perk of the job, and it was felt that this motivational factor would be diminished with the provision of all training in-house.

## 4. Conclusions

As a result of an analysis of the advantages and disadvantages of providing all training in-house, the following conclusions can be drawn:

- Considerable savings will be made in the immediate future if in-house training courses are introduced.
- The staff response is favourable overall, particularly at higher levels of management, though in some departments the loss of external training courses is seen to be a real disadvantage, with the loss of business contacts.
- While many employees feel that in-house training is a positive move and is likely to increase participation, 30% regarded it as a loss of a perk.

## 5. Recommendations

- In-house training courses should be introduced where a significant number of participants are required to attend.
- Where there are fewer than five participants, external courses should be an option.
- Staff should be consulted regularly as to the level of satisfaction with in-house training courses, and feedback regarding motivational factors should be addressed.

# 11

# Banking and finance

Finance is money used as a resource for business. The term includes references to the circulation of money, forms of credit, investments and banking facilities. This chapter focuses on banking, investments and a company's financial statements.

## Money

Below are some of the most common terms used to describe different forms of money:

| | |
|---|---|
| cash | fund |
| currency | funds |
| loan | pension |
| debt | rebate |
| fee | subsidy |
| commission | instalment |
| capital | reserves |

**cash**
money in notes and coins: *I'd like to pay in cash, please.*

**currency**
coins and banknotes of a particular country eg. dollars, yen, francs: *The pound sterling remained strong against other major currencies today.*

**loan**
money that has been borrowed and has to be paid back: *The bank agreed to give the company a loan of £50,000.*

**debt**
money owed to someone: *He was unable to pay off his debts of two million dollars.*

**fee**
payment for professional services, for example, to a lawyer,

accountant or consultant: *The fees accounted for about 20% of the total cost.*

**commission**

a payment for goods or services which is usually a percentage of the total value of a deal: *The post offers a competitive salary plus generous commission.*

**capital**

money that is used to start or expand a business: *The initial capital was raised through bank loans.*

**fund**

money or assets collected for a specific purpose and usually invested: *The money was invested in a pension fund.*

**funds**

money; financial resources: *The scheme was abandoned due to lack of funds.*

**pension**

money paid to a retired person by a company or government: *He retired with a substantial pension.*

**rebate**

part of a payment (eg. taxes) that is returned by someone official: *The tax rebate was larger than expected.*

**subsidy**

money paid by the government to producers of certain goods to allow them to sell them cheaply: *Farming has benefited greatly from subsidies.*

**instalment**

a regular part payment of a debt, usually as a means of buying goods: *We offer an instalment plan on all our white goods.*

**reserves**

profits which are not paid out to shareholders as dividends: *The company's reserves are not sufficient to fund expansion.*

## The euro

The euro is a basic monetary unit adopted by the countries of the European Union. The name 'euro' was adopted in 1995 for the European single currency and from 1 July 2002, all financial transactions must take place in euros within the Member States of the EU, with certain exceptions. Below are some facts about the euro:

- One euro consists of one hundred cents.
- The plural of 'euro' is 'euros'.
- 'euro' is written without capital letters.
- The official abbreviation for the euro is 'EUR'.
- The symbol is €.

## Bankruptcy

While some businesses perform well and expand, others are less successful and may have to stop trading and close down. The terms below are used to describe what happens to those companies that are failing:

| | |
|---|---|
| insolvent | wind up |
| creditor | receiver |
| bankrupt | liquidator |
| go bust | administrator |
| go bankrupt | voluntary liquidation |
| go into liquidation | bankruptcy |
| go into receivership | |

When a person or business is unable to pay its debts, they are considered to be **insolvent**. If the **creditors**, the people who are owed money, take the matter to court, the person or company is declared **bankrupt**. A company is then said to **go bust** (*informal*) or **go bankrupt**. At that stage a bankrupt company **goes into liquidation** (or **goes into receivership** or **is wound up**.) This process is carried out by a **receiver** (or **liquidator**, or **administrator**), a person or company appointed by the court to sell the assets of the bankrupt company, so that the creditors can be paid. Another option is for the failing company to go into **voluntary liquidation** and appoint its own liquidator. When a company is on the verge of **bankruptcy** (about to go bankrupt), it should stop trading.

*Gerry Barnes is **insolvent** so we may never see the money he owes us.*
*Ferensway Ferries was declared **bankrupt** in June.*
*The first two firms he was involved in **went bust**.*

*Unable to pay its many* ***creditors****, Maguire and Patterson* ***went into liquidation****.*
*The* ***receivers*** *have been called in at Janeway Trading Inc.*
*Business is so bad I believe they are considering* ***voluntary liquidation****.*
*Ross and Spiro is on the verge of* ***bankruptcy****.*

## Banking

A **bank** is an institution that deals in money and provides other financial services. **Banking** is the business a bank is engaged in. Here are some basic banking terms:

| | |
|---|---|
| account | charge |
| current account | ATM |
| checking account | PIN or PIN number |
| deposit account | debit |
| time or notice account | credit |
| interest | deposit |
| statement | withdraw |
| balance | |

**account**
an arrangement between a bank and a customer, allowing certain banking or credit services: *You don't need to have an account with us to apply for a credit card.*

**current account (*BrE*)**
**checking account (*AmE*)**
an account which pays little interest, but from which money can be taken out without giving notice, usually by writing a cheque (AmE *check*): *Could you let me know the balance of my current account, please?*

**deposit account**
**time** or **notice account**
an account that pays interest, but which requires notice before money can be taken out: *This deposit account offers an interest rate of 6.5%.*

**interest**
an amount that is charged for borrowing money: *Rates of interest are shown in the table on page four.*

**statement**
a document from a bank that shows transactions over a certain period: *There seems to be an error in this monthly statement.*

**balance**
the difference between money going out and money coming in at any given time: *The statement shows a balance of just $20,000.*

**charge**
an amount to be paid to a bank for providing certain services: *If you repay the full amount shown on the statement within fifteen days, there is no charge.*

**ATM**
Automated Teller Machine; a machine that dispenses cash when a card is used: *This card can be used at 4000 ATMs in the country.*

**PIN** or **PIN number**
Personal Identification Number; a number known to a card-holder which allows access to accounts through an ATM: *Your PIN will be sent to you in two or three days.*

**debit**
to deduct a sum of money from an account: *The mortgage payment will be debited from the account on the first day of the month.*

**credit**
to add an amount of money to an account: *$10,000 has been credited to the account.*

**deposit**
to put money into an account: *The sum of $5000 was deposited at the end of the month.*

**withdraw**
to take money out of an account: *How much would you like to withdraw?*

## Banking services

Commercial banks offer many services to businesses as well as to individual customers. Here are some of the most commonly used facilities:

| | |
|---|---|
| credit card | standing order |
| loan | foreign exchange |
| mortgage | insurance |
| overdraft | investment advice |
| direct debit | home banking |

A **credit card** enables the holder to buy goods and repay the credit card issuer at a later date. A **loan** is an amount of money borrowed from the bank, eg. to buy a van or pay for stock, and which must be repaid at a fixed rate of interest. A **mortgage** is a loan to buy property. Most businesses have a credit arrangement which allows them to take out more money than is in their bank account. This is called an **overdraft**.

As well as offering credit facilities, banks provide services to allow customers to make payments. **Direct debit** is a system of making payments by having money transferred from an account, eg. to pay bills. A **standing order** is an arrangement with a bank to have a fixed amount paid from a bank account to certain people or organizations at an agreed time, eg. pension scheme payments.

Most banks offer a **foreign exchange** service – the facility to change money from one currency to another, eg. Australian dollars to lira.

In recent years banks have diversified, and now offer services such as **insurance**, **investment advice** and **home-banking** (telephone and Internet) facilities.

*Our **credit card** offers flexibility and convenience throughout the world.*

*Call us to arrange a low interest **loan** to suit your business needs.*

*At this stage it makes more sense to rent premises than to take on a large **mortgage**.*

*I have a meeting with the bank manager to discuss our **overdraft**.*

*Does this account allow me to pay by **direct debit**?*

*The **standing order** will take effect from the first of June.*

*We offer a speedy **foreign exchange** service, dealing in all major currencies.*

*Could you give me some information about buildings **insurance**?*

*For **investment advice**, please call to make an appointment with one of our specialist advisers.*

*Please visit our website for more information about our **home-banking** services.*

## Types of bank

The following is a list of terms used to describe different types of bank. Note, however, that the names may vary from one country to another.

- **Central banks** such as the Bank of England (UK) or the Federal Reserve System (US) provide banking facilities for governments and other banks, as well as issuing banknotes and coins.
- **Commercial banks** are businesses that trade in money and deal directly with the public.
- A **merchant bank** specializes in raising finance for industry, arranging flotations (see page 128), takeovers and mergers (see page 10), and investment portfolios (see page 130).
- An **investment bank** is a firm that controls the issue of new securities (shares and bonds; see pages 127 and 131).
- A **clearing bank** is a bank which belongs to a clearing house (in the UK), which is an institution where members' cheques are cancelled against each other and only the balances are payable.
- A **savings bank** is a financial institution specializing in savings accounts.

> ⓘ In the UK, commercial banks are often referred to as 'High Street banks'

## The stock market

The stock market is an organized market where stocks and shares are bought and sold at prices controlled by supply and demand. The London Stock Exchange and The New York Stock Exchange on Wall Street are two of the best-known stock markets. Here are key words related to this area of finance:

| | | |
|---|---|---|
| share | listed | stockholders |
| stock | traded | dividend |
| securities | market price | stockbroker |
| quoted | shareholders | marketmaker |

A **share** (*BrE*) or **stock** (*AmE*) is any of the equal parts into which the capital of a company is divided. **Securities** are shares and bonds (official papers given by a company or the government, to prove that you have lent them money and that they will pay it back with interest). The shares of a public limited company (*BrE*) or a listed company (*AmE*) are **quoted** or **listed** on the stock exchange and can be **traded**, ie. bought and sold. The price of shares quoted on the stock exchange at a given time is called the **market price**.

The owners of a company are known as **shareholders** (*BrE*) or **stockholders** (*AmE*) and the money paid to shareholders as part of a company's profits is called the **dividend**.

People who buy and sell shares for other people and give advice on investments are called **stockbrokers**. A **marketmaker** is a wholesaler in shares who sells to stockbrokers.

***Shares*** *in the Kibazo Group fell back 95 to 667p.*
*Tesco was the most actively-traded* ***stock*** *yesterday with shares jumping to 169p.*
***Trading*** *in* ***securities*** *was brisk on the London Stock Exchange on Friday.*
*The company has been* ***quoted*** *on the stock exchange since last year, and continues to perform well.*
*It is not advisable to buy at today's* ***market price****.*
***Shareholders*** *can expect to receive a* ***dividend*** *of 5p per share.*
*He works for a firm of* ***stockbrokers*** *in Frankfurt.*
***Marketmakers*** *reported a substantial supply of new money coming into the market.*

ⓘ In British English a **stock** is a fixed-interest security issued by the government or a local authority.

## Word partnerships: share

The term **share** is commonly found preceding the words below

| | |
|---|---|
| share ... | price<br>index<br>option<br>issue<br>capital |

The value of a share is called the **share price**. Average prices of leading shares are recorded in a **share index** such as the Financial Times Stock Exchange 100-Share Index (the FTSE or 'Footsie'), or the Dow Jones Industrial Average in the Wall Street Journal. A **share option** is often offered to employees in senior management positions in a company, and allows them the right to buy shares at a reduced price. When a company offers its shares for sale to the public, this is called a **share issue**, and the money invested in a company by its shareholders is called **share capital**.

*The company blamed poor export sales for the drop in its **share price**.*
*The FTSE 100-**Share Index** hit new records yesterday.*
*Fringe benefits include **share options** and private health care.*
*The **share issue** was underwritten by ABS Investment Bank.*
*We need to increase our **share capital** in the next six months.*

## Floating a company

A private limited company which is performing well and wishes to expand may apply to the stock exchange to become a public limited company (UK) or a listed company (US). The capital which is invested by the shareholders provides the company with the funds they need to expand and diversify. When a company issues shares, ie. offers them for sale for the first time, this is known as **floating a company** or **making a flotation**. Here are the main steps involved in this process:

a company applies to the stock exchange

⇓

a bank (usually) underwrites the issue (ie. agrees to buy any unsold shares)

⇓

the company produces a prospectus, giving details of the share issue

⇓

the company issues shares

⇓

the shares are traded on the stock exchange

⇓

the shareholder receives a dividend, and can vote at the company's AGM

## The financial pages

Financial newspapers and the business sections of national newspapers provide information about world stock markets at the end of a day's trading. You can also get information through certain websites on the Internet. Here is an example from a newspaper, showing details about two companies:

**Transport**

| | | | **52-week** | | | | |
|---|---|---|---|---|---|---|---|
| **Stock** | **Price** | **Chg** | **high** | **low** | **Mkt Cap** £m | **Yld** | **P/E** |
| *NB Airlines* | 222 | +3 | 248 | 183 | 49.4 | 2.0 | 17.4 |
| *Lawson Grp* | 994 | -1.0 | 1,010 | 453 | 76.7 | 1.8 | 27.5 |

- The 'sector' indicates the part of the economy the companies belong to, eg. **transport**, mining, media, construction.

- 'Stock' heads the list of companies whose shares are listed here, NB Airlines and Lawson Group.

- The **price** shown here is the final price at the end of the previous day's trading. Prices in the examples above are given in pence (sterling).
- **Chg (Change)** indicates the change in the market price of the share from the previous day. NB Airlines' shares have gone up by 3 pence.
- The **52-week high and low** show the highest and lowest price recorded for that stock in the past 52 weeks.
- **Mkt Cap (Market capitalization)** gives the total value of a company at a given moment and is calculated by multiplying the number of shares by their market price.
- **Yld (Yield)** refers to the amount of dividend as a percentage of the share price.
- The market price of the share divided by the company's earnings (profit) per share over the last twelve month's trading is called the **P/E ratio**, the price-earnings ratio.

## Investing in the stock market

The following terms are commonly used to talk about stock market investments:

| | |
|---|---|
| portfolio | bear market |
| blue chip | institutional investor |
| speculator | mutual fund |
| bull market | unit trust |

### portfolio

a selection of investments held by an individual or organization: *Our portfolio ranges from shares in a mining company to shares in the fashion world.*

### blue chip

used to describe a large company that is considered to be a secure investment: *Telefonica is the biggest blue chip company on Madrid's stock market.*

### speculator

a person who buys and sells shares, property, currencies and commodities in order to make a profit: *Currency speculators benefited from the fall of the yen.*

**bull market**
the state of the market when prices are generally expected to rise: *The stock market had a record-breaking year in 1995 as the bull market continued its strongest performance on record.*

**bear market**
the state of the market when prices are generally expected to fall: *In a bear market investors tend to put their money into blue-chip shares.*

**institutional investor**
an organization such as a pension fund or an insurance company that holds most of the shares of leading companies: *95% of the company's institutional investors voted to pass the resolution at the AGM.*

**unit trust (*BrE*)**
**mutual fund (*AmE*)**
a company that spreads its investors' capital over a variety of securities: *Investment in a mutual fund reduces the risk for the small investor.*

## Other types of investment

Apart from stocks and shares there are many types of investment opportunities available. Here are some key words:

| | |
|---|---|
| bonds | derivatives |
| gilt-edged securities | derivative instruments |
| gilts | futures |
| treasury bonds | options |
| commodities | swaps |

When a company or government wishes to raise finance it can issue **bonds**. These are securities offered at a fixed rate of interest. Bonds issued by the government are called **gilt-edged securities** or **gilts** in the UK, and **treasury bonds** in the US.

The **commodities** market deals in items such as cereals, coffee and precious metals.

**Derivatives** or **derivative instruments** are financial products such as futures, options and swaps. **Futures** are contracts that give the right to buy and sell currencies and commodities at an agreed time in the future at a price agreed at the time of the deal. **Options** are contracts enabling the holder to buy a security at a fixed price for a limited period. **Swaps** allow the exchange of one asset for another to suit both parties, eg. currency swaps or interest rate swaps.

*He has invested heavily in **bonds** yielding 6.8%.*
*Two independent financial advisers suggested **gilt-edged securities** (**treasury bonds**) as a secure investment.*
*Coffee is considered to be the main agricultural **commodity**.*
*Speculation in **derivative instruments** such as **futures**, **options** and **swaps** has been criticized for its effects on the stock markets.*

## Financial statements

| | |
|---|---|
| accountant | turnover |
| auditor | overheads |
| profit and loss account | balance sheet |
| income statement | assets |
| revenue | liabilities |
| expenditure | cash flow statement |

By law a company has to give shareholders certain financial information. This information is compiled by the company **accountants** and verified by independent **auditors**, whose job is to check and guarantee the accounts. This is usually included in the company's annual report, and consists of three financial statements:

- **profit and loss (P&L) account** (*BrE*) or **income statement** (*AmE*). This account shows the **revenue** (money coming into the business) and **expenditure** (money going out). The **P&L** account shows the company's **turnover** (total sales), costs and **overheads**, ie. the regular costs of running a business, such as rent, salaries and electricity.

- **balance sheet**. This shows the financial situation of the company on a particular date, usually the end of the financial year. The company's **assets** (things of value belonging to the company) are recorded in the balance sheet. These include cash investments, property, and debtors (money owed by customers). Also included in the balance sheet are the company's **liabilities** – all the money that the company will have to pay out, such as taxes, mortgage, and money owed to suppliers.

- **cash flow statement** (also known as the sources and use of funds statement, and the statement of changes in financial position). This document shows the flow of cash in and out of the business, and includes sale of assets, issuing of shares, payment of dividends, trading profits and many other activities.

*He works for a firm of* ***accountants*** *in Madrid.*
*We are expecting a team of four* ***auditors*** *to be here for the whole of next week.*
*The* ***profit and loss account (income statement)*** *shows a trading profit of £86.*
*North American sales account for 80% of the company's* ***revenue****.*
*We will not be able to increase our* ***expenditure*** *on technology in the coming year.*
***Turnover*** *has been disappointingly low in the past six months.*
*Could you give me a breakdown of our* ***overheads****, please?*
*The company's* ***balance sheet*** *showed a sharp rise in borrowings.*
*All their* ***assets*** *had to be sold to pay their debts.*
*Unable to meet its* ***liabilities****, the firm was closed down.*
*His* ***cash flow statement*** *showed a number of serious errors.*

# 12

# Computers and the Internet

As computer use continues to grow and develop in all areas of life, its applications have had a great impact on the business world. One of the most important developments in computing is the Internet. This chapter looks at key words and phrases commonly used to talk about computers and the Internet. It also covers the uses of the Internet in business.

## Computers

A **computer** is an electronic machine that processes data. The term **IT** (information technology) refers to the technology of computing and telecommunications. Below is a list of words describing different types of computer:

| | |
|---|---|
| mainframe | desktop |
| minicomputer | laptop |
| workstation | notebook |
| PC | palmtop |

A **mainframe** is a powerful computer which is used in large organizations such as companies or academic institutions. It can be accessed by hundreds or thousands of users at the same time from separate computers or terminals. A **minicomputer** can support hundreds of users. A smaller, but still powerful computer is often called a workstation. A workstation is a single-user computer. A **PC** is a personal computer which is the standard computer for most individual users. There are various sizes of personal computer, including a **desktop**, and portable types such as a **laptop**, a **notebook** or a **palmtop**.

*Each computer in the university is connected to the **mainframe** computer.*
*Expanding organizations needing to make long-term plans*

*must decide whether to install **workstations** or **minicomputers**.*

*What kind of **PC** do you have?*

***Laptops**, **notebooks** and **palmtops** allow employees to keep up with paperwork and keep in touch with the office while on business trips.*

## Hardware and storage

**Hardware** is the actual machinery of a computer, the circuits, wires, and drives. Here is a list of common terms:

| | |
|---|---|
| monitor | modem |
| keyboard | scanner |
| mouse | peripherals |
| printer | |

**monitor**
the part of a computer that holds the display screen

**keyboard**
the set of keys that you use to enter information into the computer

**mouse**
a small device that controls the movement of the cursor (the small vertical line) on the screen

**printer**
a machine connected to the computer which you use to transfer information onto paper

**modem**
a device or program that enables data to be transmitted over the telephone line

**scanner**
a device that reads data from paper and enters it into the computer

**peripherals**
external devices which are attached to a computer such as printer, disk drive and keyboard, ie. all the above

**Storage** refers to the ways data can be held in the memory:

| | |
|---|---|
| disk drive | floppy disk |
| hard disk | CD-ROM |

ⓘ Floppy disks are often referred to as **floppies**.

**disk drive**
a machine that reads data from and stores data on a disk, a hard disk or a floppy disk

**hard disk**
part of a computer on which data is stored long term

**floppy disk**
a small, removable disk which is used to store data

**CD-ROM**
a plastic disk (or 'compact disk') on which data can be stored and read by a computer

## *Software and applications*

**Software** refers to all programs that are used with a computer. **Applications** are programs for specific tasks, such as compiling databases and spreadsheets (see below). Here are some basic terms:

| | |
|---|---|
| **program** | **spreadsheet** |
| **programmer** | **database** |
| **word processing** | **DTP** |

ⓘ **Program** is both a verb and a noun:
*We can program the computer to carry out this task automatically overnight.*
*They wrote a simple program to simplify the task.*

- Compare the spelling of **program** when used in computing and television:

| (BrE) | (AmE) |
|---|---|
| *a TV programme* | *a TV program* |
| *a computer program* | *a computer program* |

**program**
instructions which are written in a computer language in order to perform a task or function: *We wrote a special program to analyse the data.*

**programmer**
a person who designs and writes computer programs: *He's been a computer programmer since 1994.*

**word processing**
(often 'WP') using a computer program to create, edit, store and print a document: *Word processing is the most common of all computer applications.*

**spreadsheet**
a computer program that lets you create and manipulate rows and columns of figures: *The introduction of spreadsheets has simplified our project planning.*

**database**
a collection of information: *We have had problems with the database software.*

**DTP**
desktop publishing; producing near-professional printed matter using a PC: *The company's brochures and sales literature are produced in-house using a DTP package.*

## *Computer problems*

Some programs (called **viruses**) are deliberately designed to cause problems in a computer system. They are hidden in programs, and are not obvious to users. Here are a few of the terms you can use to talk about problems with computers:

| | |
|---|---|
| **hacker** | **bug** |
| **virus** | **debug** |
| **crash** | |

The word **hacker** means 'computer enthusiast', but it can also refer to a person who gains unauthorized access to computer systems. A **virus** is an error that is introduced into a program with the intention of causing a malfunction. A computer may **crash**, (suffer a serious failure), and stop working altogether. This may be caused by a **bug** (an error in the software). To **debug** a program or a system is to remove a bug from it.

*Police yesterday arrested a **hacker** suspected of causing computers to malfunction throughout the financial services industry.*
*A **virus** named Melissa infected all their documents.*

*Some vital files were lost when the computer **crashed**.*
*It will take us about six hours to **debug** your system.*

## Computers: verbs

The following is a list of verbs that are commonly used when talking about using computers, particularly word-processing applications. They are shown here in common partnerships.

**switch on**
to turn on (a machine or device, eg. a computer, a printer, a scanner): *Check that you've switched on the printer.*

**click (on)**
to press down on the mouse in order to select something (on the screen), eg. icons, symbols, characters: *First click on 'file', then on 'new', and then you can start typing.*

**print**
to produce a paper copy of (a document, a picture, data from a computer): *We're just about to print the final version.*

**open**
to access (files which are stored in a computer): *If you open the file called Area2, you'll get the information you need.*

**insert**
to place something (eg. text, pictures, graphics, tables, characters, paragraphs, documents) between two other items: *Once the graphics have been inserted, the report will be finished.*

**edit**
to make changes to (a document or text) by adding, rearranging or removing something: *Has the Annual Report been edited?*

**enter**
to place (data, information, pictures) in a file: *The most recent figures haven't been entered yet.*

**save**
to copy (data, files, pictures, documents) from a temporary area to more permanent storage: *Make sure you save a backup copy.*

## The Internet

With millions of users worldwide, the Internet is an exciting development for organizations and individuals alike, opening up vast resources and business opportunities, and making communication the easiest it has ever been. The terms below are commonly used to talk about the Internet:

| | |
|---|---|
| Internet | the World Wide Web |
| the Net | the Web |
| the information superhighway | WWW |
| | intranet |

The **Internet** is a worldwide network of computers which are connected by telephone lines. It is also referred to as **the Net**, and sometimes **the information superhighway**. **The World Wide Web**, also referred to as **the Web** and abbreviated to **WWW**, is the main source of information on the Net, as well as being a communication system that links users all over the world through e-mail.

An **intranet** is a network which uses the same technology as the Internet. However, an intranet is private, and can only be accessed by a particular group of people who have authorization (permission) to look at the intranet pages. Intranets are often used in business and educational contexts.

*The* ***Internet*** *has opened up vast possibilities for businesses*

*I searched* ***the Web*** *for information about employment opportunities in the finance industry.*

*The agenda for the next meeting has been posted on the director's page on the* ***intranet****.*

## *Connecting to the Internet*

Below are some terms related to gaining access to the Internet:

| | |
|---|---|
| connect to the Internet | server |
| on the Net | browser |
| online | surf the Net |
| ISP/IAP | download |

To use its resources, you need to **connect to the Internet**, be **on the Net** or be **online**. An **Internet Service Provider** (**ISP**), also called an **Internet Access Provider** (**IAP**) is a company with a large computer permanently connected to the Net. It can give users access to the Internet. Users pay to connect their computers to these large computers through a telephone line, although increasingly this service is free. Well-known examples are Demon, Virgin Net and CompuServe. A **server** is a central computer that stores and transmits documents to other computers on the network. A piece of software called a **browser** is needed to access the Internet.

Once you are connected, you can then **surf the Net** ie. move from one place to another, looking for information on the Internet. If you find something of interest you can **download** it, ie. copy a file from an online service to your own computer.

*Are you **connected to the Internet**?*

*Many banks and building societies now offer **online** accounts.*

*Are you **online** yet?*

*Many **ISPs** do not charge for access, but make their money through helplines.*

*The benefits and strengths of the **servers** that we offer depend on the conventions of the industry you work in.*

*Netscape Navigator and Microsoft Internet Explorer are examples of **browsers**.*

*The company is looking for ways to prevent employees from **surfing the Net** during working hours.*

*It was taking too long to **download** the data, so I shut down the program.*

> ⓘ The word **online** is sometimes written with a hyphen: **on-line**.
>
> - The word **website** is sometimes written as two words: **web site**.

## *The World Wide Web*

The list below shows terms which are essential for talking about the World Wide Web. These terms are explained in the next three sections:

| | |
|---|---|
| website | search engine |
| web pages | directory |
| home page | bookmark |
| hyperlink | favorite |
| HTML | domain name |
| URL | |

The information on the Web is displayed in **websites**. A website can consist of one or many **web pages**. The main page of a website is called the **home page**, which usually contains links to other pages in the site. A **hyperlink** is an element in a document that links to another place in the same document or another document.

Websites are written in **HTML**, a special programming, or 'mark-up' language.

*IT managers alone should not be responsible for the design of a company's* ***website****.*

*Companies have to allocate a budget for maintaining their* ***web pages*** *long term.*

*I feel we should redesign our* ***home page*** *as it's too complex.*

*How do I insert a* ***hyperlink*** *into a document?*

*Apart from* ***HTML****, which programming languages can you use?*

## How to find information on the Web

Once you are connected to the Internet, you can look for information in an organized or more random way, depending on your needs. Here are some suggestions to start you off.

- Open up your browser, eg. Microsoft Internet Explorer or Netscape Navigator.
- Finding the site you need:

  If you know of a site you want to see, type in the web address (**URL**) and click 'enter'. You will be connected to the website you want.

  You can also use a **search engine**. A search engine is a facility which enables you to find information by searching for 'keywords'. Some well-known search engines are Alta Vista, Lycos and Hotbot. Type in a keyword and the search engine will present you with a list of sites which you can choose from.

  Finally, you can use a **directory**, which is similar to a search engine but has categories you can choose from. Yahoo! and Infoseek are popular directories.
- You can mark websites by using **bookmarks**, or **favorites** in your browser. This facility allows you to make a personalize collection of the addresses of sites you visit frequently.
- Use the **hyperlinks** in the web pages to help you move to areas of the site or other sites.

## Web addresses

It is essential to type a web address correctly, using UPPER or lower case letters as necessary. If you make a mistake with any of the parts of the address, it may not be recognized. There should not be any spaces between the different parts of the address. The

An example of a page from a company's website

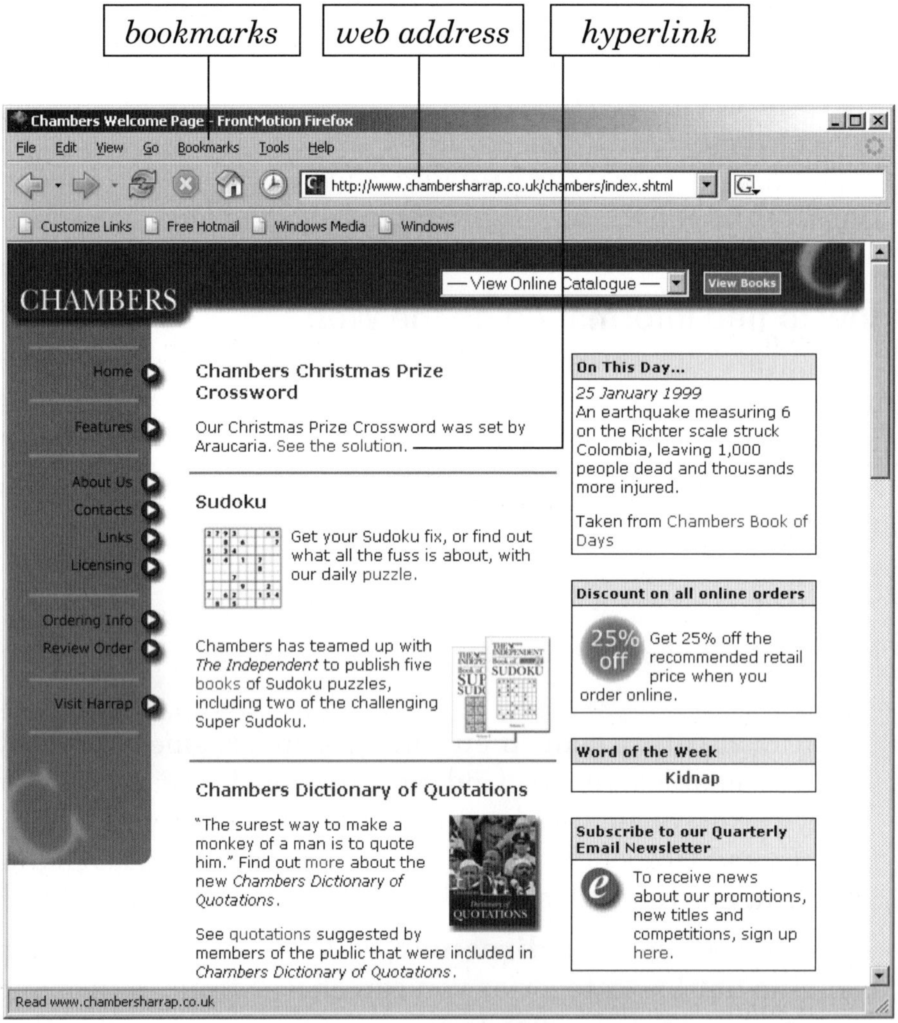


term **domain name** describes the part of the URL that includes the establishment and the country name. In the example below, the company is Electronic Share Information and the country is the UK.

Individual letters of a web address are pronounced separately: a web address such as **www.esi.co.uk** is pronounced:

*'double-u double-u double-u dot ESI dot koh dot UK'*

## *E-mail*

The most widely-used function on the Internet is e-mail (electronic mail). E-mail allows users to send and receive text, graphics, sounds and animated images, and has become an alternative to conventional mail, telephone and fax. Not only is it cheap and easy to use, but it also provides a record of communications sent and received. In business, e-mail provides cheap and rapid communication between the employees of an organization, and between a company and its clients and suppliers.

| | |
|---|---|
| e-mail address | check your e-mail |
| e-mail account | attachment |
| e-mail program | |

People need your **e-mail address** in order to send messages to your account.

**E-mail programs** such as Pegasus Mail or Microsoft Outlook enable you to read your messages.

When you want to know if you have received any messages, you **check your e-mail**.

You can send files such as word-processed documents or spreadsheets with your e-mail. A file sent like this is called an **attachment**.

*Could you tell me your* ***e-mail address*** *please?*
*Can you access your* ***e-mail account*** *from any computer?*
*Which* ***e-mail program*** *do you have?*
*I'll be with you when I've* ***checked my e-mail****.*
*I'll send you the report as an* ***attachment****.*

ⓘ All of the following spellings are possible: **e-mail**, **email**, **Email** or **E-mail**.

- **E-mail** is also a verb:
  *Could you e-mail me the details?*

## *E-mail addresses*

An e-mail address contains an **identifier**, ie. your name or nickname. After that comes the symbol '@' (pronounced 'at'), followed by the **domain name**, which identifies the server that is used to send your mail, the category of organization and the country code (if it is not the United States). The different elements of the domain name are separated by dots. Note that there are no spaces between the characters, and there is no full stop at the end.

Example: **al.davidson@hawks.co.uk**

| **al.davidson** | **@** | **hawks** | **.co** | **.uk** |
|---|---|---|---|---|
| identifier | 'at' symbol | name of organization | type of organization | country |

- This e-mail address is said in the following way:
  ***al dot davidson, at hawks, dot co, dot UK***
- The abbreviation for the country name is said as separate letters. For information on writing e-mails, see chapter 9, page 107.

## *Doing business on the Internet*

As well as having a presence on the Web, companies can use it to access the growing number of websites of interest. Below are outlined some of the ways in which businesses can benefit from its functions. The following terms are explained in this section:

| | |
|---|---|
| e-commerce | banner (ad) |
| encryption | keyword advertising |
| e-cash | |

- **e-mail**
  Businesses use this form of communication to deal with customers, to make and respond to enquiries quickly, and to communicate with employees.
- **the corporate website**
  A corporate website may be used for publicity, for selling, or for sharing information.
- **e-commerce**
  **E-commerce** or 'online trading' has proved to be very successful for some companies. For example, an increasing number of banks provide online accounts to their customers.

One of the advantages of this form of trading is that users can come to the website twenty-four hours a day. However, security is a concern for many consumers. With developments in **encryption** (putting letters and numbers into code so that they cannot be understood) and **e-cash** (digital cash), payment solutions are likely to be less of a problem in the future.

- **marketing and advertising**
  Marketing on the Web can be achieved by setting up a website and making it attractive to visitors. It can also be done by taking out advertisements on other companies' websites. This kind of advertisement is called a **banner** or **banner ad**. Displaying advertisements on the results pages of a search is called **keyword advertising**.

- **searching for and gathering information**
  The Internet is a powerful tool for gathering data. Companies can use it to look up other companies and their products, consult databases, access financial information, find market information, foreign exchange rates and so on.

- **video-conferencing**
  Using computer networks to transmit audio and video data between two or more people in different locations is a time-saving method of communication.

- **recruitment**
  Many companies place their recruitment needs on their own websites or on the websites of recruitment agencies.

- **investor relations**
  Large corporations are moving towards placing their annual reports on their websites in order to provide a service to their shareholders.

***E-commerce*** *is becoming recognized as a major online service, and provides lower transaction costs for the company.*

***Encryption*** *allows credit card users to feel more confident about security when making electronic payments.*

***E-cash*** *is one of the payment solutions explored by banks and software houses.*

***Banner ads*** *and* ***keyword advertising*** *allow a company to target its audience on the Internet.*

# Appendix A

# Abbreviations

This list contains abbreviations commonly used in business contexts.

| | |
|---|---|
| @ | at |
| a/c | account |
| AGM | Annual General Meeting |
| am | ante meridiem; before noon; morning |
| AOB | Any Other Business |
| approx. | approximately |
| APR | Annual Percentage Rate |
| asap | as soon as possible |
| attn. | attention |
| b/d | banker's draft |
| B/E | bill of exchange |
| CAD | computer-aided design |
| cc | copies to |
| C&F | cost and freight |
| CEO | Chief Executive Officer |
| c/f | carried forward |
| CIF | cost, insurance, freight |
| c/o | care of |
| Co | company |
| COD | cash on delivery |
| cont'd | continued |
| CV | curriculum vitae |
| DD | direct debit |
| del | delivery |
| dept. | department |
| Dir | Director |
| DP | data processing |
| ea. | each |
| e.g. | for example |
| e-mail | electronic mail |
| encl. | enclosed |
| ETA | estimated time of arrival |
| EU | European Union |

| | |
|---|---|
| FOB | free on board |
| fwd | forward |
| GDP | gross domestic product |
| GNP | gross national product |
| HQ | headquarters |
| i.e. | that is |
| ILO | International Labour Organization |
| IMF | International Monetary Fund |
| Inc. | Incorporated |
| incl. | including |
| j.i.t. | just in time |
| K | thousand |
| L/C | letter of credit |
| Ltd | limited |
| MBA | Master of Business Administration |
| misc. | miscellaneous |
| N/A | not applicable |
| no. | number |
| OHP | overhead projector |
| p.a. | per annum; per year |
| P&L | profit and loss |
| PC | personal computer |
| Pd | paid |
| P/E | price/earnings |
| plc, PLC, Plc | public limited company |
| p&p | postage and packing |
| pp | on behalf of |
| PR | public relations |
| PTO | please turn over |
| Pty | proprietary company |
| Pte | private limited company |
| p.w. | per week |
| qty | quantity |
| R&D | research and development |
| re | regarding; about |
| ref | reference |
| ROI | return on investment |
| s.a.e. | stamped addressed envelope |
| SE | stock exchange |
| tba | to be announced |
| V.A.T. | value added tax (UK) |
| WP | word processing |
| WWW | World Wide Web |

# Appendix B

# Numbers

It is important to be able to say and understand numbers in business contexts. You may need to give or receive details over the phone or during a face-to-face discussion. Remember to ask for clarification and check that you have received or have given the right numbers.

## Pronunciation

Be careful of the difference in pronunciation between numbers like thirteen and thirty; nineteen and ninety etc. Misunderstandings could cause problems.

### *The number 0*

We say **zero**, **oh** or **nought**.

**Zero** can be used to talk about any kind of number:

| | |
|---|---|
| 0.25 | *zero* point two five |
| Tel: 305 6670 | three *zero* five six six seven *zero* |
| Room 702 | seven *zero* two |

You can also use **nought** before a decimal point and **oh** after it.

| | |
|---|---|
| 0.56 | *nought* point five six |
| 0.202 | *nought* point two *oh* two |

**Oh** is also used in telephone and fax numbers, room numbers, reference numbers and account numbers. (See **Dates**)

| | |
|---|---|
| 3460928 | three four six *oh* nine two eight |
| Room 6065 | six *oh* six five |
| Ref number 3408 | three four *oh* eight |

### *Telephone and fax numbers*

Say each digit separately, except for 'doubles' which you can join together.

| | |
|---|---|
| 210485 | two one oh four eight five |
| 471 661 | four seven one *double six* one *or* four seven one *six six* one |

We often group the digits, putting a slight pause between the groups, as this makes it easier to say and to understand the number.

| | |
|---|---|
| 21 34 85 | two one, three four, eight five |
| 213 485 | two one three, four eight five |

Note that it is *not* usual to say *twenty-one, thirty-four, eighty-five* in English.

## Decimals

In British English it is usual to say each individual digit after the decimal point. This is not the case in American English.

| | **BrE** | **AmE** |
|---|---|---|
| 4.56 | four point five six | four point fifty-six |
| 0.175 | nought point one seven five | zero point one hundred seventy-five |

Note that in English we use and say **point** for decimals, not **comma**.

## Hundreds, thousands, millions and billions

| | |
|---|---|
| 100 | a hundred |
| 250 | two hundred and fifty |
| 1000 | a thousand |
| 5400 | five thousand, four hundred |
| 10,650 | ten thousand, six hundred and fifty |
| 100,000 | a hundred thousand |
| 240,000 | two hundred and forty thousand |
| 500,000 | five hundred thousand (or half a million) |
| 1,000,000 | a million |
| 1,000,000,000 | a billion |

- In American English, **and** is not used after hundred:

  367 is *three hundred sixty-seven*
- Note that hundred, thousand, million and billion do not take a plural when they are used with precise numbers:

  *six hundred and eighty-five* (no 's' on the hundred)
- Hundred, thousand, million, billion take a plural when they are used with imprecise numbers:

*Hundreds of people arrived for the conference.*
*Thousands of our customers are in the Far East.*

- A comma, rather than a full stop, indicates thousands and millions:
  *31,000* not *31.000*

## Dates

There are various ways to write dates, but to avoid confusion write the month as a word rather than a number.

| **Write** | **Say** |
|---|---|
| 1 October 1999 | the first of October nineteen ninety-nine |
| October 1, 1999 | October the first, nineteen ninety-nine. |
| 1875 | eighteen seventy-five |
| 1904 | nineteen oh four *or* nineteen hundred and four |
| 2000 | two thousand |
| 2004 | two thousand and four |

## Other numbers

| | |
|---|---|
| 20% | twenty per cent |
| ½ | a half |
| ¾ | three quarters *or* three fourths (*AmE*) |
| 3 ½ | three and a half |

# Index